A Taste of Christmas

A Treasury of
Holiday Recipes, Menus, Customs, Crafts and Gift-Giving Ideas

We wish to thank all of our friends and relatives who have shared their recipes and encouraged us to write this book. A very special thank you to our husbands, Craig, Ed and Bill for all their support.

by Jacquie Schmit ❊ Eileen Mandryk ❊ Jo Wuth

Front Cover Photograph – Holiday Sugar Cookies, page 40, Gingerbread Cookies, page 42

A Taste of Christmas
by
Jacquie Schmit ✾ *Eileen Mandryk* ✾ *Jo Wuth*

Third Printing – November 1998

Three Sisters Publishing
12234 – 49 Street
Edmonton, Alberta
Canada T5W 3A8
website: www.3sistersbook.comm

CANADIAN CATALOGUING IN PUBLICATION DATA
Schmit, Jacquie
    A taste of Christmas
    Includes index.
    ISBN 1-895292-85-9

1. Christmas cookery.   2. Christmas decorations.
3. Christmas.   I. Mandryk, Eileen
II. Wuth, Jo   III. Title.
TX739.2.C45S35   1997   641.5'68   C97-920061-X

Photography by:
Merle Prosofsky, Merle Prosofsky Photography, Edmonton, Alberta

Gingerbread House and Christmas Cookie Decoration by:
Susan Wuth

Dishes and Accessories courtesy of:
The Bay
Call the Kettle Black,The High Street, Edmonton, Alberta

Seafood courtesy of Fin's Seafood Distributors, Sherwood Park, Alberta

Designed, Printed and Produced in Canada by:
Centax Books, a Division of PrintWest Communications Ltd.
Publishing Director, Photo Designer & Food Stylist: Margo Embury
1150 Eighth Avenue, Regina, Saskatchewan, Canada S4R 1C9
(306) 525-2304   FAX (306) 757-2439

Table of Contents

Homespun Christmas 5
(Candy & Gift-Giving Ideas)

Yule Love It.. 25
(Cakes, Cookies & Squares)

Why Not Brunch 69
(Brunch Dishes, Breads & Muffins)

Holiday Cheer.. 95
(Beverages)

Merry Beginnings.. 101
(Appetizers & Soups)

Yuletide Feasts 113
(Salads, Vegetable Dishes & Main Dishes)

Sweet Endings 153
(Desserts)

Holiday Menu Suggestions.. 164
(Holiday Season Parties and Dinners)

Index.. 168

Recipes have been tested in U.S. Standard measurements. Common metric measurements are given as a convenience for those who are more familiar with metric. Recipes have not been tested in metric.

Feelings of Christmas

Sleigh bells ringing
Choirs singing
The glisten of freshly fallen snow,

Gingerbread baking
Children aching
To see Santa with his cheeks aglow,

Dancing Christmas lights
Stars shining bright
Families skating on a frozen pond,

Soft candle glow
Falling snow
Friends and family gathering to bond,

The fragrance of pine
Children looking to find
Gaily wrapped gifts under the tree,

Peace on earth
good will to all men
This is what Christmas means to us three.

by Eileen Mandryk for the sisters three

We were born and raised the Campbell girls in the farming community of Lamont, Alberta. Our parents always made Christmas a very special, magical time of the year for us, so it is only natural that our first book is for the Christmas holiday season. It is our hope that you will enjoy these recipes as we do, and that some of them may become part of your Christmas traditions.

Enjoy and Merry Christmas from the Three Sisters.

Homespun Christmas

Candy
Gift-Giving Ideas

Sugar Plums

Variations of these delectable sugared fruits have been around for generations – remember the Sugar Plum Fairy from The Nutcracker ballet and the visions of sugar plums from the classic 'Twas the Night Before Christmas. Now you can make your own!

½ cup	dried apricots	125 mL
½ cup	pecans	125 mL
⅓ cup	angel flaked coconut	75 mL
¼ cup	golden raisins	60 mL
¼ cup	dried apples	60 mL
2 tbsp.	any fruit liqueur	30 mL
	icing sugar	

In a food processor fitted with steel blade, finely chop the apricots, pecans, coconut, raisins and dried apples. With the motor running, add the desired liqueur and blend the mixture for 5 seconds. Form the mixture into ¾" (2 cm) balls, pressing each candy firmly into shape. Sift icing sugar into a bowl and roll the sugar plums in the sugar to coat them evenly. Store in an airtight container. They can be kept up to 2 weeks at room temperature or can be frozen for several months.

Makes approximately 32 sugar plums

Gift Suggestion: Small tins or glass jars make good gift containers. Add a plaid ribbon around each jar top for a holiday look.

 Christmas Gift Wrapping

Until the late 1800s, Christmas gifts were usually just placed on the floor beneath the Christmas tree or tied, unwrapped, to the tree. In the 1880s, gifts were wrapped in white paper and brightly colored ribbons or gold or silver cords were tied around them. In the early 1900s, specially printed papers with Christmas images were produced for wrapping Christmas gifts.

Marzipan Kartoffel

(German Marzipan Potatoes)

10 oz.	almond paste OR marzipan, diced	285 g
⅔ cup	icing sugar	150 mL
½ cup	cocoa powder	125 mL

On a work surface, sprinkle almond paste with sugar. Gently work with hands until smooth. Do not overwork. Taste; add more sugar, if desired. Divide mixture into thirds; shape each into a long roll. Divide each roll into 10 equal pieces. Roll pieces into ¾" (2 cm) diameter balls. Roll balls in cocoa, coating thoroughly; tap off excess. If desired, place in tiny paper or foil cups. Store in an airtight container.

Makes about 30 balls

Marzipan Fruits, Vegetables and Figures

Marzipan, a delicious mixture of almonds and sugar flavored with rose water or orange juice was brought to Europe by the Arabs. Known in Persia over 1,000 years ago, it became a great delicacy for Christmas feasts, wedding banquets and even royal gifts. Marzipan, traditionally shaped in the form of tiny fruits and vegetables, has been an important part of German Christmas traditions. It was used as Christmas tree ornaments and as a prized gift.

In Scandinavian traditions, a beribboned marzipan pig is often the reward for the lucky child who finds the almond hidden in the traditional Christmas Eve rice porridge. Large three-headed marzipan dragons filled with dried fruits are a Spanish Christmas tradition. Some pastry shops feature menageries of fanciful marzipan animals, colored with vegetable dyes.

Children and adults can create imaginative marzipan ornaments. Work marzipan and sugar as in the marzipan recipe above or start with marzipan recipe page 90; add more icing sugar if it is too sticky. Shape marzipan into fruits, vegetables, fanciful animals or figures. Brush marzipan shapes with diluted food coloring, using water color brushes. For more intense color, work paste food colors into the marzipan. Set decorated shapes aside to dry.

Turkish Delight

As pretty as it is delicious, this Middle Eastern specialty
adds a colorful sparkle to a sweet tray.

3 tbsp.	gelatin	45 mL
½ cup	cold water	125 mL
2 cups	sugar	500 mL
½ cup	hot water	125 mL
1	orange, grated rind and juice of	1
1	lemon, grated rind and juice of	1
	red, green OR orange food coloring	

In a small bowl, soften gelatin in cold water. In a saucepan, make a syrup of sugar and hot water, place over medium heat and bring to a boil. Boil gently for 20 minutes; remove from heat and add softened gelatin; add strained fruit juices, rind and red, green or orange food coloring. Pour into an 8" (20 cm) square pan that has been rinsed with cold water. When firm, cut into squares with a knife dipped in hot water.

Makes 24 pieces

Pictured on page 17.

Gift Suggestion: Save interesting packages and containers throughout the year, e.g., rounds of Brie often come in flat, round wooden containers, perfect for gifts of candies and cookies. Line with tissue paper and decorate with ribbon around the edge or tie with ribbon and add a Christmas bauble or pretty card.

Christmas Carols

For many centuries, Christmas carols have enhanced the joy and spirit of Christmas. In 1521 the first known collection of Christmas carols was printed. Contemporary collections of carols date largely from the 1700s, 1800s and 1900s. Today, traditional and modern carols are sung throughout the Christmas season in many countries around the world.

Aunt Susie's Coconut Candy

Our Aunt Susie was a very special aunt who always graced our Christmas holidays with an array of tempting homemade candy. This recipe was our favorite and the one she became most noted for.

2 cups	shredded coconut, finely chopped	500 mL
2 cups	sugar	500 mL
¼ cup	light corn syrup	60 mL
½ cup	water	125 mL
½ tsp.	vanilla	2 mL
4 x 1 oz.	squares semisweet chocolate	4 x 30 g

Chop coconut finely. Combine sugar, syrup and water in a large saucepan. Set over medium-high heat and bring to a boil, stirring constantly. Continue boiling until mixture reaches the soft-ball stage, 238°F (114°C). Remove from heat; add coconut and vanilla; stir until creamy. Turn onto a smooth flat surface and, with a rolling pin dusted with icing sugar, roll into a thin sheet about ⅜" (1 cm) thick. Melt 2 squares of chocolate over hot water; pour the chocolate evenly over the candy. Allow chocolate to harden, then flip candy over and repeat with chocolate. Cut into squares when chocolate is cool and hard.

Makes about 60 pieces

 # Christmas Bells

Ringing out the bells at Christmas is a tradition that began centuries ago. On Christmas Eve in medieval times, the bells in churches tolled to warn the devil of the coming birth of Jesus, who would save the world from darkness. For an hour before midnight the mournful tolling continued and then, at the stroke of midnight, a triumphant, happy pealing of the bells announced the death of Satan and the birth of the Savior. Today bells not only ring out from churches, but are found as a symbol throughout holiday decorations, including tree ornaments, door wreaths, as wrapping paper design, on napkins, name tags, and even miniature bells tied on gifts. Perhaps most beautiful of all are the bells that peal on Christmas morning announcing the birth of the Savior.

Chocolate Truffles

These rich, creamy chocolates are ideal for gift giving.

Ganache Filling:

1 cup	whipping cream	250 mL
½ lb.	semisweet chocolate	250 g
2 tbsp.	chocolate liqueur OR 1 tsp. (5 mL) vanilla	30 mL
	icing sugar	

Chocolate Coating:

¾ lb.	semisweet chocolate	375 g
1 cup	cocoa powder	250 mL

Ganache Filling: In a small saucepan, heat cream to scalding point (bubbles form around edge of pan); remove from heat. Stir in semisweet chocolate until smooth; stir in liqueur. Transfer to a bowl; cover and refrigerate for 1 hour, or until thickened and cold. Using a whisk (not an electric mixer), beat chocolate mixture just until creamy and lighter in color. Do not overbeat or mixture will separate. Shape ganache into small balls about 1" (2.5 cm) in diameter and place on waxed paper-lined baking sheets. Cover and refrigerate for 30 minutes, or until firm. Working with balls of filling, lightly roll them in icing sugar. Between your fingertips, gently roll each ball to round them off. Return them to the waxed paper-lined sheet and freeze for about 1 hour, or until hard and almost frozen.

Chocolate Coating: In the top of a double boiler over hot (not boiling) water, melt semisweet chocolate. Remove from heat and let cool slightly. Sift cocoa into a pie plate. Using 2 forks, dip balls into chocolate, letting excess drip off. (If chocolate thickens, rewarm gently over hot water.) Place each ball in cocoa powder. Using 2 clean forks, roll truffles in cocoa. Refrigerate on a waxed paper-lined baking sheet until hard. Place truffles in a covered container and store in refrigerator until just before serving. Refrigerate truffles for up to 1 week or freeze for up to 3 months.

Makes about 36 pieces

Chocolate Truffles

Continued

Variations:

👫 *Chocolate Orange Truffles:* When making the filling, substitute orange-flavored liqueur or orange juice for chocolate liqueur; add 1 tbsp.(15 mL) finely grated orange rind. Do not roll chocolate-coated truffles in cocoa. Garnish with thin curled strips of orange rind just before serving.

👫 *Hazelnut Truffles:* When making the filling substitute hazelnut liqueur for chocolate liqueur, add ½ cup (125 mL) ground hazelnuts. Roll chocolate-coated truffles in 2 cups (500 mL) finely chopped toasted hazelnuts instead of cocoa.

🎄 The Christmas Tree 🎄

According to historical accounts, the first mention of Christmas trees is in stories recorded in Latvia and Estonia in the early 1500s where, after festive Christmas Eve dinners, formally dressed members of the local merchants' guild placed a decorated evergreen tree in the town square, proceeded to dance around it and then set it on fire.

Nevertheless, it is Germany that developed the Christmas tree tradition we know today. An old travel diary from Strasbourg tells of fir trees set up and decorated with brightly colored paper roses, apples and gilded candies and nuts.

From France in 1708 comes the description of a Christmas tree decorated with lighted candles fastened to each branch, and with new clothes, silver, dolls and sugar candy placed beneath it for each child.

Christmas Rum Balls

These creamy, moist balls are very "rummy",
an attractive addition to your sweet tray.

2 cups	semisweet chocolate chips	500 mL
½ cup	almond paste	125 mL
1 cup	sour cream	250 mL
4 oz.	cream cheese, softened	125 g
⅛ tsp.	salt	0.5 mL
8 cups	vanilla wafers, finely crushed (may use ½ graham crumbs)	2 L
3 cups	icing sugar	450 mL
⅔ cup	cocoa powder	150 mL
2 cups	finely chopped pecans	500 mL
1 cup	melted butter	250 mL
1-1½ cups	white rum	250-375 mL
	chocolate sprinkles	

In a saucepan, melt chocolate chips and add almond paste, sour cream, cream cheese and salt. Combine well and set aside. In a separate bowl, combine wafer crumbs, icing sugar, cocoa and finely chopped pecans. Add melted butter and rum; mix until it holds its shape, then add the chocolate-sour cream mixture. Blend well; you may have to knead with your hands until the mixture is blended and soft. Chill dough in refrigerator until firm enough to hold shape. Form into balls and roll in chocolate sprinkles. Place on cookie sheets and refrigerate overnight to harden. Place Rum Balls in containers and store in refrigerator for approximately 2 weeks, until they mature. When serving, take out of refrigerator about 4 hours before serving time. If kept longer than 4 weeks, Rum Balls should be frozen.

Makes approximately 80-90 balls

Gift Suggestions: Pack rum balls in small boxes lined with clear or colored cellophane. Decorate the wrapped boxes with small pine cones or holly sprigs. Save interesting boxes throughout the year.

Almond Roca

*Crunchy buttery almond candy smothered in chocolate –
a joy to eat or to give as a gift.*

2 cups	butter	500 mL
2 cups	brown sugar	500 mL
¼ cup	water	60 mL
2 tbsp.	light corn syrup	30 mL
2 cups	slivered almonds	500 mL
8 x 1 oz.	squares semisweet chocolate	8 x 30 g

Melt butter in a heavy saucepan over low heat. Add sugar and stir constantly until sugar is dissolved. Add water and corn syrup. Continue cooking over low heat until it reaches 290°F (143°C) or hard crack stage*. Stir frequently but slowly to prevent scorching. Remove from heat with as little agitation as possible. Stir in 1⅓ cups (325 mL) of almonds. Chop remaining almonds. Pour into a 9 x 13" (23 x 33 cm) pan (a shallow pan to depth of ¼" [1 cm]). Melt half the chocolate and cool slightly. Pour a thin layer of chocolate over the almond crunch. Sprinkle half the remaining nuts over the warm chocolate. Allow chocolate to harden, then turn over and repeat the coating process. Break coated roca into pieces and store in covered container in the refrigerator.

Makes about 48 pieces

* At hard-crack stage, the hot syrup, when dripped into cold water, separates into brittle threads.

Pictured on page 17.

 Decorating Suggestions: For a festive-looking dessert buffet table, tie ribbons around the stems of clear or colored champagne glasses. Coordinate lace, tartan, or gold or silver ribbons or cords to your decor. Fill the dishes with truffles, rum balls, Noël Nuts, etc.

Chocolate Almond Bark

A favorite year round, Chocolate Almond Bark seems especially delicious as a holiday treat.

| 8 x 1 oz. | squares semisweet chocolate | 8 x 30 g |
| ½ cup | whole blanched toasted almonds | 125 mL |

Cut each square into 4 pieces. Partially melt chocolate over hot, not boiling, water, stirring constantly until chocolate is two-thirds melted. Remove from heat and continue stirring until completely melted. Stir in almonds. Spread on waxed paper-lined baking sheet. Chill until firm. Break into pieces. Store in refrigerator.

Makes about 8 oz. (250 g) of Almond Bark

Variations:

To make **White Chocolate Almond Bark**, use white chocolate instead of semisweet, in which case you would use only 6 squares. For other variations, any kind of toasted nuts or chopped dried fruit or nut/fruit combination may be substituted for almonds. Try **Chocolate Hazelnut Apricot Bark.**

To make a dramatic-looking **Marbled Bark**, use 4 squares of semisweet or bittersweet chocolate and 4 squares of white chocolate. Melt chocolate as above in 2 separate bowls. Stir half of the nuts or fruit into each batch of chocolate. Drop alternating spoonfuls of white and dark chocolate on a waxed paper-lined baking sheet. Draw a knife through the chocolate to create a marbled look. Finish the recipe as above.

Gift Suggestions: Save small boxes throughout the year. Line them with foil, fill with Chocolate Almond Bark, and wrap them with decorative fabrics or with foil; add a Christmas seal or small ornament as a finishing touch.

Noël Nuts

Sugar 'n' spice and everything nice, these easy-to-make candied pecans are sweet Christmas snacks.

1	egg white	1
1 tsp.	cold water	5 mL
4 cups	large pecan halves	1 L
½ cup	sugar	125 mL
¼ tsp.	salt	1 mL
½ tsp.	cinnamon	2 mL
⅛ tsp.	nutmeg	0.5 mL

Beat egg white and water until frothy. Add pecans and mix until well coated. Combine sugar, salt, cinnamon and nutmeg. Add to pecan mixture. Spread on buttered cookie sheet. Bake at 225°F (107°C) for 1 hour, stirring every 15 minutes. Remove from oven and cool completely. Store in a covered airtight container up to 4 weeks.

Makes 4 cups (1 L)

 Gift Suggestion: Noël Nuts make great gifts packaged in decorative tins or in glass jars with pretty lids. If the glass jars have metal lids, tie fabric caps and ribbons over the lids.

Dilly Dilly Crackers

These zesty little tidbits were a big hit at our family Christmas last year at Mom Schmit's. The recipe comes from Jacquie's mother-in-law, Joan.

1 oz.	pkg. Ranch Dressing mix	28 g
2 tsp.	dillweed	10 mL
½ cup	vegetable oil	125 mL
4 oz.	box Ritz Bits mini crackers	250 g

In a large bowl, combine the dressing mix, dillweed and oil. Stir to combine. Add the mini crackers and stir well to combine. This will keep for up to 2 weeks stored in an airtight container.

Makes 4 cups (1 L)

Nuts and Bolts

Every Christmas, Shelley, Eileen's daughter, makes these for family and friends. This recipe is from her mother-in-law, Pat.

3 cups	EACH Crispix cereal, Cheerios, spoon-sized shredded wheat	750 mL
2 cups	EACH pretzel sticks and mini rounds	500 mL
1 cup	mixed nuts	250 mL
2 cups	vegetable oil	500 mL
1 tbsp.	EACH seasoning salt, onion powder	15 mL
2 tsp.	EACH garlic powder, celery salt	10 mL
2 tsp.	Worcestershire sauce	10 mL

Preheat oven to 250°F (120°C). Combine cereals, pretzels and nuts in a large roaster. Mix well. Combine all other ingredients; stir well. Drizzle over the cereal mixture; mix well. Roast, uncovered, for 1½ hours, stirring every 20 minutes. Remove from oven; let cool completely. Store in airtight containers for up to 1 month.

Makes 4 quarts (4 L)

Baked Caramel Corn

6 qts.	popped popcorn	6 L
1 cup	butter OR margarine	250 mL
2 cups	brown sugar	500 mL
½ cup	corn syrup	125 mL
1 tsp.	salt	5 mL
½ tsp.	baking soda	2 mL
1 tsp.	vanilla	5 mL
	nuts (optional)	

Keep popcorn warm at 300°F (150°C). Melt butter; add sugar, syrup and salt. Bring to a boil, stirring constantly. Boil for 5 minutes without stirring. Remove from heat; stir in baking soda and vanilla. Remove popcorn from oven; add nuts if using. Pour caramel into popcorn, stirring well. Spread over 2 baking pans. Bake at 250°F (120°C) for 1 hour; stir every 15 minutes. Cool; break apart; store in airtight tins.

Makes 5 quarts (5 L)

Pictured opposite.

Homespun Christmas

(Candy & Gift-Giving Ideas)

left to right:
   Cappuccino Mix, page 19
   Raspberry Vinegar, page 22
   Almond Roca, page 13
   Dog Bones, page 23
   Hot Pepper Oil, page 22
   Baked Caramel Corn, page 16
   Strawberry Champagne Jelly, page 20
   Raspberry Wine Jelly, page 20
   Turkish Delight, page 8

Almond Vanilla Coffee

1 cup	ground coffee (not instant)	250 mL
½ cup	coarsely ground almonds	125 mL
1	whole vanilla bean, minced	1
1 tsp.	freshly ground nutmeg	5 mL
⅛ tsp.	almond extract	0.5 mL

Combine all ingredients. Use the coffee in any drip or filter coffee maker at 1½ times the normal strength. Use within 2 weeks.

Yields approximately 16 cups (4 L) of brewed coffee

Cappuccino Mix

1 cup	instant coffee creamer	250 mL
1 cup	instant chocolate drink mix	250 mL
⅔ cup	instant coffee	150 mL
½ cup	sugar	125 mL
½ tsp.	cinnamon	2 mL
¼ tsp.	ground nutmeg	1 mL

Place all the ingredients in a blender or food processor and process until finely powdered. Store in an airtight container. To use, stir 3 tbsp. (45 mL) of the mix into 6 oz. (175 mL) of hot water.

Makes approximately 12 cups (3 L) of coffee

Pictured on page 17.

Mocha Coffee

½ cup	EACH instant coffee, sugar and coffee creamer	125 mL
2 tbsp.	cocoa powder	30 mL

Place all ingredients in a blender or food processor and process until finely powdered. To serve, place 2 heaping teaspoons (15 mL) in 1 cup (250 mL) of boiling water, or to taste.

Makes approximately 8 cups (2 L) of coffee

 Gift Suggestion: Package any of these coffee mixes attractively in pretty glass jars or decorative tins with a card giving instructions for serving.

Strawberry Champagne Jelly

A taste of the "rich and famous" for breakfast!

2 cups	frozen strawberry beverage base	500 mL
1½ cups	champagne OR other sparkling wine	375 mL
1 cup	water	250 mL
4 cups	sugar	1 L
6 oz.	liquid fruit pectin	170 mL

Sterilize jars or other glass containers with boiling water; keep jars warm.

Combine strawberry concentrate, champagne, water and sugar in a deep heavy saucepan. Heat to boiling over high heat, stirring constantly to dissolve sugar. Stir in pectin and bring to a full rolling boil (liquid will continue to boil hard even when stirred). Boil hard 1 minute while stirring. Remove from heat, let stand a few minutes then skim off foam with a metal spoon. Pour jelly into warm jars. After a few minutes, skim again. Seal at once with a thin layer of hot paraffin or use jars with 2-piece lids. Let set undisturbed for about 12 hours.

If using wine glasses or other decorative containers without lids, cool until set then cover tightly with a circle of plastic wrap and refrigerate. Jelly should be used within a few weeks.

Makes about 7½ cups (1.75 L) of jelly

Variation:

Raspberry Wine Jelly: Substitute frozen raspberry beverage base for strawberry and use 3 cups (750 mL) white or rosé wine instead of champagne. Increase sugar to 6 cups (1.5 L) and use 12 oz. (340 mL) of liquid fruit pectin.

Pictured on page 17.

Antipasto

Very flavorful, serve this chunky, colorful spread with assorted crackers.

1	large head cauliflower, cut into bite-sized pieces	1
2	large red bell peppers, cut into small pieces	2
3	medium green bell peppers, cut into small pieces	3
2 x 10 oz.	cans button mushrooms, drained	2 x 284 mL
14 oz.	can pitted black olives, drained	398 mL
12 oz.	jar stuffed green olives, drained	375 mL
2 x 8 oz.	jars sweet pickled onions, drained and chopped	250 mL
26 oz.	jar garlic dill pickles, drained and chopped	750 mL
2 x 6½ oz.	cans tuna in oil, drained	2 x 198 g
2½ cups	ketchup	625 mL
10 oz.	bottle chili sauce	285 mL
14 oz.	can tomato sauce	398 mL
1 cup	vinegar	250 mL
1 cup	vegetable oil	250 mL
2 x 4 oz.	cans broken shrimp, rinsed and drained	2 x 113 g

Cut cauliflower and peppers into small pieces. Drain all vegetables, olives and pickles. Cut mushrooms in half, quarter olives and onions. Thinly slice dills. Break tuna into small chunks. Combine ketchup, chili sauce, tomato sauce, vinegar and oil in a large saucepan. Bring to a slow boil. Meanwhile, steam cauliflower and peppers for 2 minutes; rinse with cold water. Drain very thoroughly and immediately stir into hot sauce. Add all remaining ingredients and bring quickly to the boil. Pour into sterilized jars and seal. Process in boiling water bath for 20 minutes for half pints (250 mL) and 30 minutes for pints (500 mL). Store in the refrigerator for 1 week or freeze if not using immediately.

Makes approximately 20 half pints (20, 250 mL jars)

Hot Pepper Oil

Use very sparingly in stir-fries or salads to liven them up.

2 cups	canola oil	500 mL
½ cup	crushed dried hot red peppers	125 mL
4 tsp.	peppercorns	20 mL
	small dried whole hot peppers	

In a small heavy saucepan, heat oil with the crushed red peppers over low heat until candy thermometer registers 180°F (82°C) and bubbles rise to the surface. Remove oil from heat; let stand for 12 hours. Strain oil through a fine sieve into a bowl, pressing to extract as much oil as possible. Divide peppercorns among small sterilized bottles; add 1 whole hot pepper to each. Pour oil through a coffee filter-lined funnel into bottles; seal with corks. Oil can be stored in the refrigerator for up to 4 weeks. Makes 1½-2 cups (375-500 mL) of oil.

Pictured on page 17.

Raspberry Vinegar

This red fruity vinegar will put zest into a salad dressing. Wonderful as a gift.

6 cups	frozen raspberries (2 x 10½ oz. [300 g] pkgs.)	1.5 L
3 cups	white wine vinegar OR rice vinegar	750 mL
2 tsp.	granulated sugar	10 mL
	whole raspberries, fresh OR thawed	

In a food processor, chop together frozen raspberries, vinegar and sugar. Transfer to a large microwaveable bowl. Cover, microwave at medium high for 7 minutes, or heat on the stove top over medium heat for 10 minutes. Refrigerate for 12 hours, stirring occasionally. Strain vinegar through a fine sieve into a bowl, pressing to extract all liquid. Line funnel with coffee filter or double thickness of rinsed fine cheesecloth; place in a clean dry bottle. Pour in raspberry vinegar; let stand until completely filtered; top up filter and change bottles as necessary. It takes about 8 hours for the filtering and straining process. Add 3 raspberries per bottle; seal with corks. Store in a cool, dark, dry place. Makes about 5 cups (1.25 L)

Pictured on page 17.

Dog Bones

*A homemade Christmas treat for your family pet or
for a surprise gift idea for a friend's or neighbor's pet.*

2 cups	flour (white OR brown)	500 mL
½ cup	wheat germ	125 mL
½ tsp.	salt	2 mL
1 tsp.	brewers' yeast	5 mL
½ cup	dry milk powder	125 mL
4 tbsp.	chilled bacon drippings	60 mL
¼ cup	shredded Cheddar cheese	60 mL
1	egg	1
½ cup	water	125 mL

In a large bowl, mix flour, wheat germ, salt, yeast and dry milk. Stir
with a fork to combine. Add and cut in the fat and cheese as you would
for pie crust. Beat egg and stir into this mixture. Add water, stirring
only until you can gather the mixture into a stiff dough. Knead
2-3 minutes, until smooth, and roll to ½" (1.3 cm) thickness. Cut with a
bone-shaped cookie cutter. Bake on greased cookie sheets at 325°F
(160°C) for 25 minutes, or until brown.

Makes 12-16 bones, depending on the size of the cookie cutter

Pictured on page 17.

Christmas Tree Tips

Keep the tree outdoors until you are ready to decorate it. ♣ Cut off
at least 1" (2.5 cm) of the trunk; cut straight across. ♣ Use a sturdy
tree stand with a large water basin and feed the tree fresh water every
day. ♣ Add a commercial tree preservative or make your own using
1 part 7-Up (not diet) to 3 parts water. To 4 quarts (4 L) of this mixture
add 1 or 2 drops of chlorine bleach – to prevent bacteria build up.
Don't use more bleach or the tree may suffer.

Cinnamon Craft Ornaments

To create ornaments with a wonderful holiday scent,
use the following recipe to make simple decorations.

1 cup	cinnamon	250 mL
1 tbsp.	EACH ground cloves, nutmeg	15 mL
¾ cup	applesauce	175 mL
2 tbsp.	tacky glue	30 mL

In a plastic container, combine dry ingredients. Stir in applesauce and glue. Work mixture with hands for 2-3 minutes to form a ball. If dough is too dry, add more applesauce; if it is too wet, add more cinnamon. Knead the dough on a surface sprinkled with cinnamon. The dough should have a pasty consistency like clay. Divide dough into 4 equal portions. Roll out dough to ¼" (1 cm) thickness. Cut dough with cookie cutters or omit the rolling and shape dough with your hands. Use a straw to poke a hole into the top of each ornament. Let ornaments dry completely before hanging.

Christmas Dough Ornaments

Create dough ornaments for your Christmas tree or as special
decorations for your Christmas parcels.

1 cup	flour	250 mL
½ cup	salt	125 mL
½ cup	water	125 mL
	acrylic paints and paintbrushes	
	ribbon, cord OR string	

In a small bowl, combine flour, salt and water to make a soft dough. Divide dough in half. Wrap one half of dough in plastic and knead remaining dough on a floured surface until smooth, 8-10 minutes. Roll dough to ¼" (1 cm) thickness. Cut out shapes with a cookie cutter or omit the rolling and shape dough with your hands. Place ornaments on a foil-lined cookie sheet. Using a straw, poke a hole into the top of each ornament. Bake at 250°F (120°C) for 4-5 hours, until completely dry. Let cool. Paint cooled ornaments and let dry. Use ribbon, cord or string to hang ornaments.

Yule Love It

Cakes

Cookies

Squares

Traditional Old-Fashioned Scots' Plum Pudding

1 cup	fine dry bread crumbs	250 mL
½ cup	flour	125 mL
½ lb.	seeded raisins*	250 g
½ lb.	currants*	250 g
½ lb.	seedless raisins*	250 g
½ lb.	suet, finely chopped	250 g
1 tsp.	cinnamon	5 mL
½ tsp.	ground nutmeg	2 mL
½ tsp.	ground mace	2 mL
½ tsp.	salt	2 mL
½ cup	chopped blanched almonds	125 mL
1 cup	mixed peel	250 mL
5	eggs, separated	5
¼ cup	brandy	60 mL

Combine all ingredients, except eggs and brandy, and mix well. Beat egg whites until stiff. Beat egg yolks until thick and lemon colored. Mix egg yolks and brandy into the fruit mixture. Fold in egg whites carefully. Pack into 3 or 4 well-greased, heat-proof bowls or molds. Cover the tops so that water does not get into the pudding. You can butter waxed paper and place on top of bowl; tie a string around the paper, then cover again with foil. Place molds on a rack in a Dutch oven or roaster. Add boiling water to come a quarter of the way up the sides of the mold. Simmer, covered, adding more boiling water as necessary. Steam 6 hours for large and 4-4½ hours for smaller puddings. When cooked, remove puddings from molds and cool. Wrap well in waxed paper and then foil. Puddings may be stored in the refrigerator for 3-4 weeks or frozen.

To reheat, wrap in waxed paper and then wrap tightly in foil. Place in the top of a double boiler and steam for 1½-2 hours. Serve hot with Caramel Sauce, page 28, or Traditional Hard Sauce, page 29.

* Thoroughly wash and dry before using.

Note: If seeded raisins are not available, use all seedless.

Makes 3 or 4 puddings and serves 10-12 per mold

Mom's Steamed Carrot Christmas Pudding

Every October, while Mom was preparing the Christmas Pudding, it was a tradition that every member of the family would take a turn stirring the pudding. As you stirred, you were to make a wish for the coming year. When the pudding was packed into the molds, Mom would wrap coins and buttons in waxed paper and insert them into the puddings. The buttons signified the recipient would be a bachelor or spinster; the coins meant riches and wealth. Flaming the pudding is optional, but it makes a spectacular presentation.

1 lb.	EACH seeded and seedless raisins, washed and dried, OR all seedless	454 g
1 lb.	grated carrots	454 g
1 lb.	mixed peel	454 g
1 lb.	beef suet, finely chopped	454 g
1 loaf	white bread, crumbled OR bread crumbs	1 loaf
1 tsp.	EACH nutmeg, cloves and cinnamon	5 mL
6	eggs	6
1 tsp.	almond extract	5 mL
¼ cup	rum OR brandy for flaming (optional)	60 mL

In a large bowl, combine all ingredients, except for eggs, almond extract and rum or brandy. Mix well. Beat eggs; add almond extract; add to mixture. Mix all together well. Pack into 3 or 4 well-greased, heat-proof bowls or molds. Cover the tops so that water does not get into the pudding. Butter waxed paper and place on top of bowls; tie a string around the paper; cover again with foil. Place molds on a rack in a Dutch oven or roaster. Add boiling water to ¼ of the way up the sides of molds. Simmer, covered, add more boiling water as necessary. Steam 6 hours for large and 4-4½ hours for smaller puddings. When cooked, remove from molds and cool. Wrap well in waxed paper and then foil. Puddings may be stored in refrigerator for 3-4 weeks or frozen. To reheat, rewrap in waxed paper and foil. Place in top of double boiler and steam for 1½-2 hours. To flame the pudding, warm rum or brandy in a small saucepan; do not boil. Ignite warm rum with a long match; pour flaming rum over the pudding. Serve hot with the Caramel Sauce, page 28, or one of the other sauces on page 29.
Serves 10-12 per mold

Pictured on page 51.

Caramel Sauce for Carrot or Plum Pudding

¼ cup	flour	60 mL
1 cup	brown sugar	250 mL
¼ cup	butter	60 mL
2 cups	boiling water	500 mL
1 tsp.	vanilla	5 mL
2-3 tbsp.	brandy (optional)	30-45 mL

In a small bowl, combine the flour and brown sugar; mix well. In a saucepan over medium heat, melt butter; whisk in the flour and sugar mixture and cook, stirring constantly for 1-2 minutes. Add the boiling water gradually, stirring constantly until mixture is thickened and smooth. Remove from heat and stir in vanilla and brandy, if using. Serve hot over pudding slices.

Makes enough for 12 servings

Pictured on page 51.

Old-Fashioned Orange Sauce

½ cup	brown sugar, packed	125 mL
2 tbsp.	cornstarch	30 mL
1 tbsp.	grated orange rind	15 mL
¼ tsp.	salt	1 mL
1½ cups	water	375 mL
2 tbsp.	butter	30 mL
1	orange, juice of, OR ¼ cup (60 mL) of Grand Marnier OR any other orange liqueur	1

In a heavy saucepan, stir together sugar, cornstarch, orange rind and salt; stir in water and bring to a boil, stirring constantly. Reduce heat to low and stir in butter and orange juice or liqueur. Simmer for 2 minutes. Serve hot over pudding slices.

Makes approximately 2 cups (500 mL)

Traditional Hard Sauce

Mound the hard sauce in a pretty bowl; chill the sauce and spoon it over hot or cold Christmas puddings. The British call this Brandy Butter, but try the other flavorings too.

4-5 tbsp.	butter	60-75 mL
1 cup	icing sugar	250 mL
⅛ tsp.	salt	0.5 mL
1 tbsp.	brandy OR strong coffee, rum, Grand Marnier, lemon juice OR 1 tsp. (5 mL) vanilla	15 mL
¼ cup	cream (optional)	60 mL

Beat butter until soft; gradually add sugar and beat until fluffy. Beat in salt and brandy or other flavorings. Beat in cream if using. Chill thoroughly.

Makes about ½ cup (125 mL) of sauce

Variations:

- *Spiced Hard Sauce:* add ½ tsp. (2 mL) cinnamon or nutmeg and ¼ tsp. (1 mL) cloves.
- *Brown Sugar Hard Sauce:* substitute brown sugar for white sugar and use all or part of the cream.

Creamy Custard Sauce

3 tbsp.	sugar	45 mL
1¾ cups	half and half cream	425 mL
1	egg yolk	1
1 tbsp.	cornstarch	15 mL
⅛ tsp.	salt	0.5 mL
½ tsp.	vanilla	2 mL

In a heavy saucepan, combine all ingredients except vanilla. Cook over medium heat, stirring constantly until mixture coats the back of a spoon, about 10-15 minutes. Remove from heat; stir in vanilla. Chill.

Makes 1½ cups (375 mL)

Amaretto Fruit Cake

The delicate flavor of Amaretto enhances this rich, moist light fruit cake.

1½ cups	golden raisins, washed and dried	375 mL
4 oz.	candied citron peel	115 g
8 oz.	candied red cherries	225 g
4 oz.	candied green cherries	115 g
8 oz.	candied yellow pineapple	225 g
¼ cup	brandy	60 mL
¼ cup	Amaretto	60 mL
½ cup	flour	125 mL
4 oz.	whole blanched almonds	115 g
½ cup	butter	125 mL
½ cup	margarine	125 mL
1 cup	sugar	250 mL
4	eggs	4
¼ cup	brandy	60 mL
¼ cup	Amaretto	60 mL
1 tsp.	almond flavoring	5 mL
2½ cups	flour	625 mL
¼ cup	milk	60 mL
2 oz.	ground almonds (½ cup [125 mL])	55 g

Place raisins, peel and whole cherries in a large bowl. Cut pineapple into ½" (1.3 cm) pieces and add to fruit mixture. Pour ¼ cup (60 mL) each of brandy and Amaretto over top. Mix thoroughly, cover and leave overnight.

Grease a 6½" (16 cm) and a 5" (13 cm) round fruit cake pan, or any suitable baking pans that will hold at least 12 cups (3 L) of batter. Line the pans with waxed paper and grease the paper.

Preheat oven to 275°F (140°C). Sprinkle ½ cup (125 mL) flour over the fruit mixture and toss to coat fruit. Mix in whole almonds.

Amaretto Fruit Cake

Continued

Place ½ cup (125 mL) each of butter and margarine in a large mixing bowl. Beat together until creamy. Gradually beat in the sugar and continue beating until light and fluffy. Add eggs, one at a time, beating well after each addition, then add the brandy, Amaretto and flavoring. Add about ¾ cup (175 mL) of flour, beating just until mixed. Beat in the milk and another ¾ cup (175 mL) of flour. Stir in the ground almonds and remaining flour. Pour over the fruit and nut mixture and stir until combined. Turn into the prepared cake pans and smooth the top. Place a pan containing water on the bottom rack of the oven. Bake cakes in the center of a preheated 275°F (140°C) oven for 2-3 hours, or until a cake tester inserted into the center comes out clean. Remove cakes from oven; let cool in pans on a rack for 15-20 minutes. Remove from pans; peel off paper and cool completely. Wrap cakes well and let ripen for 3-4 weeks in refrigerator or freeze.

Makes 2 round cakes or 2-3 loaves

Christmas Pudding

To some, especially those with English ancestry, Christmas dinner wouldn't be complete without a blazing Christmas pudding for dessert. Historians tell us that in the 18th century, plum pudding was served as a first course – stirred by each member of the family for good luck and cooked five weeks prior to Christmas, on Stir-Up Sunday, the Sunday before Advent. Originally made with plums, Christmas pudding is now usually made with suet, currants, raisins, nuts and spices. Carrot pudding is also often served as a Christmas pudding. Warmed brandy or rum is used to flame the pudding and holly is a traditional garnish.

Light Coconut Fruit Cake

Aunt Rene, a favorite aunt, and our Mother's twin sister, shared many of her recipes with us. This moist chewy light fruit cake is one of them. All coconut lovers will appreciate this.

2 lbs.	sultana raisins, washed and dried	1 kg
½ lb.	candied citron peel	225 g
½ lb.	candied cherries	225 g
½ lb.	whole blanched almonds	225 g
¼ cup	brandy	60 mL
2½ cups	flour	625 mL
1 cup	butter	250 mL
2 cups	sugar	500 mL
6	eggs	6
1 tsp.	almond extract	5 mL
1 tsp.	vanilla	5 mL
4 tsp.	baking powder	20 mL
1 lb.	angel flaked coconut	500 g
14 oz.	can crushed pineapple and juice	398 mL

Preheat oven to 275°F (140°C). Combine raisins, peel, cherries and almonds in a large bowl. Pour brandy over fruit mixture and mix thoroughly. Sprinkle with 1 cup (250 mL) of the flour and toss to coat fruit and nuts. Cream butter, and gradually beat in the sugar, eggs and flavorings. Combine 1½ cups (375 mL) flour, baking powder and coconut. Add half of the flour mixture to the butter mixture, beating just until mixed. Beat in the crushed pineapple and then the remaining flour mixture. Pour over the fruit and nut mixture and stir until combined well. Turn into 2 or 3 loaf pans that have been greased, lined with waxed paper, and greased again. Place a pan containing water on the bottom rack of the oven. Bake cake for 2-3 hours, or until cake tester inserted into center comes out clean. Remove from oven; let cool in pans on a rack for 15-20 minutes, then remove from pans and peel off paper. Cool loaves completely and wrap well. Store in refrigerator or freeze.

Makes 2-3 loaves

Everyday Fruit Cake

This easy recipe makes a moist, light fruit cake that is wonderful for Christmas or any time all year round.

8 oz.	whole blanched almonds	250 g
1 lb.	sultana raisins, washed and dried	500 g
4 oz.	candied citron peel	115 g
4 oz.	candied red cherries	115 g
4 oz.	candied green cherries	115 g
4 oz.	candied pineapple	115 g
3 cups	flour	750 mL
1 cup	butter	250 mL
2 cups	brown sugar	500 mL
5	eggs	5
1 tsp.	vanilla	5 mL
1 tsp.	almond extract	5 mL
1 tsp.	baking powder	5 mL
1 cup	orange juice	250 mL

Place almonds, raisins, peel and cherries in a large bowl. Cut pineapple into ½" (1.3 cm) pieces and add to fruit mixture. Sprinkle ½ cup (125 mL) of the flour over the fruit and nut mixture and toss to coat fruit.

Grease 2 or 3 loaf pans. Line the pans with waxed paper and grease the paper. Preheat oven to 275°F (140°C).

In a large mixing bowl, cream the butter. Gradually beat in the sugar, eggs and then the flavorings. Combine 1¼ cups (300 mL) of flour and baking powder; beat into butter mixture until just mixed. Beat in the orange juice and then the remaining 1¼ cups of flour. Pour over the fruit and nut mixture and stir until combined. Turn into the prepared cake pans and smooth the top. Place a pan containing water on the bottom rack of the oven. Bake cake for 2-3 hours, or until a cake tester inserted into the center comes out clean. Remove from oven; let cool in pans on a rack for 15-20 minutes. Remove cake from pans and peel off paper. Cool completely, wrap well and refrigerate or freeze.

Makes 2-3 loaves

Dark Fruit Cake

1½ lbs.	currants	750 g
2 lbs.	raisins	1 kg
2 lbs.	candied cherries, halved	1 kg
1½ lbs.	candied pineapple, chopped	750 g
½ lb.	EACH dates, mixed peel, citron	250 g
1 lb.	pecans	500 g
½ cup	brandy to soak fruit in (optional)	125 mL
4 cups	flour	1 L
2 cups	white sugar	500 mL
1 lb.	butter	500 g
10	eggs	10
1 tsp.	EACH cloves, nutmeg, allspice, salt	5 mL
2 tsp.	cinnamon	10 mL
1 tsp.	baking soda	5 mL
1	lemon, juice and rind of	1
1	orange, juice and rind of	1
¾ cup	grape juice	175 mL
¼ cup	brandy	60 mL
½ cup	molasses	125 mL

Wash currants and raisins and dry well; chop fruit and nuts; mix together and add ½ cup (125 mL) of brandy, if using; stir well; allow to stand overnight if brandy is used. Dredge fruit and nuts in half the total amount of flour and allow to stand at least 8 hours.

Preheat oven to 250°F (120°C). Grease 4, 5 x 9" (13 x 23 cm) loaf pans well, line them with waxed paper and grease well again. Cream sugar and butter; add eggs and mix well; add all remaining ingredients and combine well. Pour batter over floured fruit and nut mixture and combine well. Fill pans no more than three-fourths full. Put a pan of water on the bottom rack of the oven. Bake cake for 1½-2 hours, or until a cake tester inserted into the center comes out clean. Take loaves out of the oven and remove from the pans. Let loaves cool on cake rack until cold. Wrap well and refrigerate for up to 1 month or freeze.

Makes 4 loaves

Pictured on page 51.

Mom's Traditional Christmas Cake

A delicious moist orange, almond-flavored light fruit cake.

2 cups	sultana raisins, washed and dried	500 mL
1 cup	candied red cherries	250 mL
1 cup	candied green cherries	250 mL
1½ cups	chopped candied pineapple	375 mL
2½ cups	mixed candied fruit	625 mL
1 cup	candied citron peel	250 mL
1½ cups	chopped blanched almonds	375 mL
2 cups	flour	500 mL
½ cup	butter	125 mL
1 cup	sugar	250 mL
3	eggs	3
1 tbsp.	grated orange rind	15 mL
1 tsp.	almond extract	5 mL
½ tsp.	salt	2 mL
2 tsp.	baking powder	10 mL
½ cup	orange juice	125 mL

In a large bowl, combine raisins cherries, pineapple, mixed fruit, peel and almonds; toss with ½ cup (125 mL) of the flour and set aside.

In large bowl, beat butter with sugar until light and fluffy; beat in eggs, one at a time. Add orange rind and almond extract and beat well. Combine remaining flour, baking powder and salt. Add flour mixture alternately with orange juice, making 3 additions of dry and 2 additions of liquid. Mix just until flour is blended. Fold in fruit mixture.

Preheat oven to 250°F (120°C). Grease 2, 5 x 9" (13 x 23 cm) loaf pans. Line pans with a double thickness of waxed paper and then grease paper. Spoon batter into pans and smooth tops.

Set a shallow pan of boiling water on the bottom rack of the oven. Bake cakes for 2½ hours, or until cake tester inserted into center comes out clean. Let cakes cool completely in pans on racks. Remove from pans and wrap well. Refrigerate for up to 1 month or freeze.

Makes 2 cakes

Pictured on page 51.

Traditional Scottish Dundee Cake

This is an old Scottish family favorite. This classic Scottish fruit cake traditionally has the top completely covered with almonds.

2½ cups	flour	625 mL
1 tsp.	baking powder	5 mL
½ tsp.	salt	2 mL
1 cup	sultana raisins, washed and dried	250 mL
1 cup	currants, washed and dried	250 mL
½ cup	chopped candied orange and lemon peel	125 mL
1 cup	butter	250 mL
1 cup	sugar	250 mL
5	eggs	5
½ cup	whole blanched almonds	125 mL
1 tbsp.	grated orange rind	15 mL
2 tbsp.	orange juice	30 mL
¼ tsp.	almond extract	1 mL

Combine the flour, baking powder and salt. Mix in raisins, currants and chopped peel. Cream butter and sugar well. Beat in eggs one at a time. Grind almonds in a blender or food processor and add to butter mixture. Combine well. Stir flour mixture into butter mixture, mixing well. Add the grated orange rind, orange juice and almond extract. Mix well. Preheat oven to 275°F (140°C). Turn into 2 or 3 small loaf pans that have been greased, lined with waxed paper, and greased again. Place a pan containing water on the bottom rack of the oven. Bake cake for 1-1½ hours, or until cake tester inserted into center comes out clean. Remove from oven; let cool in pans on a rack for 15-20 minutes, then remove from pans and peel off paper. Cool completely and wrap well. Store in refrigerator or freeze.

Makes 2-3 loaves

Cherry Bundt Cake

The rich cherry flavor makes this cake hard to resist and the bundt shape makes a festive presentation. Garnish with holly sprigs for a dessert buffet table.

1½ cups	sugar	375 mL
8 oz.	cream cheese, softened	250 g
1 cup	butter OR margarine	250 mL
1½ tsp.	vanilla	7 mL
4	eggs	4
2¼ cups	sifted cake flour	550 mL
1½ tsp.	baking powder	7 mL
¾ cup	well-drained maraschino cherries	175 mL
½ cup	chopped pecans	125 mL

Icing Sugar Glaze:

1½ cups	icing sugar	375 mL
2 tbsp.	milk	30 mL

cherries and nuts for garnish (optional)

Preheat oven to 325°F (160°C). In a large mixing bowl combine sugar, cream cheese, butter and vanilla, mixing until well blended. Add eggs, one at a time, mixing well after each addition. Gradually add 2 cups (500 mL) of cake flour sifted with baking powder. Mix well. Toss remaining ¼ cup (60 mL) of flour with cherries and chopped nuts. Fold into the batter. Grease a 10" (25 cm) bundt pan; pour batter into pan. Bake for 1 hour and 20 minutes to 1½ hours, or until cake tester inserted into the center comes out clean. Cool on a wire rack for 5 minutes, remove from pan. Cool thoroughly.

Combine icing sugar and milk; mix well and drizzle over cake. Garnish with additional cherries and nuts, if desired.

Serves 15-20

Old-Fashioned Carrot Cake

The combination of cinnamon, nutmeg, ginger and applesauce make this cake moist and flavorful.

3 cups	flour	750 mL
1 cup	sugar	250 mL
1½ tbsp.	ground cinnamon	22 mL
½ tsp.	ground nutmeg	2 mL
2 tsp.	baking soda	10 mL
1 tsp.	baking powder	5 mL
1 tsp.	salt	5 mL
½ tsp.	ground ginger	2 mL
1½ cups	unsweetened chunky applesauce	375 mL
1¼ cups	vegetable oil	300 mL
1 cup	brown sugar	250 mL
1 tbsp.	vanilla	15 mL
4	eggs	4
2 cups	shredded carrot (about 4 medium carrots)	500 mL
1 cup	chopped walnuts	250 mL

Preheat oven to 350°F (180°C). In a large bowl, mix flour, sugar, cinnamon, nutmeg, baking soda, baking powder, salt and ginger. In a medium bowl with a wire whisk or fork, beat applesauce, vegetable oil, brown sugar, vanilla and eggs until smooth. Stir applesauce mixture, shredded carrots and walnuts into flour mixture, just until flour is moistened. Pour batter into a greased 10" (25 cm) springform pan and bake for 65-70 minutes, or until a toothpick inserted in center of cake comes out clean. Cover the top of the cake with foil if it browns too quickly. Cool cake in pan on a wire rack 10 minutes; remove sides of pan and cool cake completely on rack. When cake is cool, remove bottom of pan, and place cake on a serving plate. Frost with the following cream cheese frosting.

Serves 20-25

Cream Cheese Frosting

8 oz.	cream cheese	250 g
6 tbsp.	softened butter OR margarine	90 mL
1 tsp.	vanilla	5 mL
1½ cups	icing sugar	375 mL

In a large bowl, with mixer at medium speed, beat cream cheese, butter and vanilla until blended. Gradually beat in icing sugar until smooth.

Makes enough to frost 1 cake

Holiday Spritz Cookies

A rich "melt-in-your-mouth" traditional German cookie.

1 cup	golden-flavored shortening	250 mL
½ cup	sugar	125 mL
1	egg	1
1 tsp.	vanilla	5 mL
½ tsp.	almond extract	2 mL
2¼ cups	flour	550 mL
¾ tsp.	salt	3 mL

Preheat oven to 400°F (200°C). In a large bowl combine shortening, sugar, egg, vanilla and almond extract. With electric mixer at medium speed, beat until mixture is light and fluffy. Add flour and salt and beat at low speed until mixture is combined and smooth. Place dough in a cookie press. Press into desired shapes on an ungreased baking sheet. Bake for 5-7 minutes, or until set but not brown. Remove cookies from oven and place on wire rack to cool. Store in airtight containers and freeze for up to 3 months.

Makes approximately 60 cookies

Note: Dough can be tinted with a few drops of food coloring. If using colored sugar crystals, sprinkle on before cookies are baked. If decorating with icing, do so after cookies are cooled. See pages 40 and 41.

Holiday Sugar Cookies

These rich holiday classics can be made well in advance.

1 lb.	butter	500 g
2½ cups	icing sugar, sifted	625 mL
1 tbsp.	vanilla	15 mL
2	eggs	2
5 cups	flour	1.25 L
1 tsp.	baking soda	5 mL
1 tsp.	salt	5 mL

Cream butter with sugar; beat in vanilla and eggs. Combine flour, baking soda and salt. Blend gradually into creamed mixture. Divide dough in half and chill. Dough can be shaped into a roll about 2" (5 cm) in diameter and sliced about ¼" (6 mm) thick; or dough can be rolled out and cut into shapes with cookie cutters. Preheat oven to 350°F (180°C). Place cookies on ungreased baking sheets. Bake for about 8-12 minutes depending on thickness. Cool slightly before removing from pan, then cool completely on wire racks. Ice or decorate as desired. Store in airtight containers and freeze for up to 3 months. See decorating suggestions and icing recipes below and on pages 41 and 42.

Makes 84 cookies

Pictured on the front cover.

To Decorate Cookies & Houses

Put each icing color in a different piping (pastry) bag.

To make colored sugars, use ¼ tsp. (1 mL) food coloring powder to 1 cup (250 mL) granulated sugar. Use a separate bowl for each color and add more food coloring for more intense colors.

Sprinkle colored sugar on wet icing; after icing has dried, shake off loose sugar.

To paint with icing, put Royal Icing in a small bowl and thin to heavy cream consistency with water. Use pastry brush for large flat areas or a small watercolor brush for detail on cookies or gingerbread houses.

Royal Icing

This icing is traditionally used for decorating gingerbread houses and people or sugar cookies. Keep it covered with a damp towel or plastic wrap as it dries out quickly.

3	egg whites	3
4 cups	icing sugar	1 L
½ tsp.	cream of tartar	2 mL
	lemon juice OR water as needed	
	food coloring (optional)	

In a deep bowl, beat egg whites until stiff, but not dry. Gradually add icing sugar and cream of tartar, beating for about 1 minute more, until icing is of spreading consistency. Add lemon juice or water to thin icing, if necessary. Add more sugar to thicken.

Makes about 2 cups (500 mL)

To color icing:

To keep icing white, add a drop of blue food coloring. Keep white portion separate from icing to be tinted other colors. Use paste colors for the most intense icing color.

Icing Paint

This quick and easy version makes cookie decorating fun for children.

4 cups	icing sugar	1 L
⅓ cup	water OR more as needed	75 mL
	food coloring	

Combine icing sugar and water, adding more water as needed to make a spreadable consistency. Divide icing into separate bowls and tint with food color paste. Thin with water as needed. Keep icing bowl(s) covered with a damp towel or plastic wrap.

Makes about 2 cups (500 mL)

Gingerbread Cookies

Delicious cookies, gingerbread people or gingerbread houses can be created from this easy recipe. Use cardboard cutouts for gingerbread house patterns.

3½ cups	flour	875 mL
1 tsp.	baking soda	5 mL
1½ tsp.	EACH ginger, cinnamon	7 mL
1 tsp.	ground cloves	5 mL
½ cup	butter OR margarine	125 mL
¾ cup	sugar	175 mL
1	egg, unbeaten	1
¾ cup	molasses	175 mL
2 tsp.	grated orange rind	10 mL

Combine flour, baking soda, ginger, cinnamon and cloves; set aside. Cream together butter and sugar, add egg, molasses and orange rind; beat well. Add flour mixture and mix thoroughly. Refrigerate overnight. Preheat oven to 375°F (190°C). Roll out dough on a floured surface to a ¼" (6 mm) thickness. Cut gingerbread into desired shapes and place on a greased cookie sheet. Bake for 10-12 minutes. Remove from oven and place on a wire rack to cool. Ice or decorate as desired. Store in airtight containers and freeze for up to 3 months.

Makes approximately 36 cookies

Cookies pictured on the front cover; Gingerbread House pictured on the back cover.

To Decorate Gingerbread Cookies:

If the gingerbread people or cookies are going to be used as Christmas tree decorations, use a plastic drinking straw to punch holes in the top of each cookie before baking. Thread ribbons through the holes to hang the decorated cookies.

Use Royal Icing or Icing Paint, page 41, to create imaginative and beautiful cookies to decorate your tree or a Christmas cookie platter or to give as gifts.

Star or snowflake cookie cutters come in various sizes. Use a small star to cut out the center of a large cookie star to create a delicate effect. Outlines and beads of royal icing, dotted with silver dragées, can create decorative gingerbread ornaments.

Brune Kager

(Danish Spice Cookies)

Danish cooks are rated on how thin they make their Brune Kager – some cooks even mix their batter 2 weeks in advance of baking the cookies, to ensure the flavors are well blended.

1 cup	butter	250 mL
1 cup	sugar	250 mL
½ cup	corn syrup	125 mL
2¾ cups	flour	675 mL
1 cup	chopped almonds	250 mL
1 tbsp.	cinnamon	15 mL
2 tsp.	ground ginger	10 mL
2 tsp.	ground cloves	10 mL
1 tsp.	baking soda	5 mL

In a large bowl, beat butter with sugar until creamy; stir in corn syrup. Combine flour, almonds, cinnamon, ginger, cloves and baking soda; with a wooden spoon, gradually stir into butter mixture to make a soft, but not sticky, dough. Divide dough into 4 portions. On a lightly floured surface, roll each portion into a 1½" (4 cm) diameter log. Wrap in plastic wrap and refrigerate until chilled. Preheat oven to 400°F (200°C). Cut rolls into ¼" (1 cm) thick slices; place slices on greased baking sheets and bake for 8-10 minutes, or until golden brown. Let cool on pans for 3 minutes. Remove to racks to let cool completely. Store in airtight containers and freeze for up to 3 months.

Makes about 8 dozen

Variation:
Dough may be rolled out and cut into shapes with cookie cutters.

Kanel Kakor

These crisp, spicy Swedish cinnamon wafers are hard to resist.

1 cup	butter OR margarine	250 mL
1 cup	sugar	250 mL
1	egg, separated	1
2 cups	flour	500 mL
2 tbsp.	cinnamon	30 mL
	slivered almonds	

Preheat oven to 350°F (180°C). In a large bowl, cream butter; beat in sugar until light and fluffy. Gradually beat in egg yolk. Stir in flour and cinnamon, mixing well. Shape dough into a rectangle. Turn a 10 x 15" (25 x 38 cm) jelly-roll pan upside down. Grease pan bottom and place dough in the center. Cover with waxed paper. Roll out dough to cover entire surface, distributing evenly and smoothly. With a sharp knife, trim excess from sides of baking sheet. Beat egg white slightly until foamy and brush over surface, coating thoroughly. With pastry wheel or sharp knife, cut dough into 3 equal strips lengthwise and 16 strips across. Place an almond in the center of each wafer. Bake for 15-18 minutes, or until evenly browned. With a spatula, carefully separate strips and place on a wire rack to cool. Store in airtight containers and freeze for up to 3 months.

Makes 48 cookies

Swedish Christmas Traditions

Light and food are the highlights of Swedish Christmas festivities. Early on Saint Lucia's Day, December 13, little girls, with candle-studded crowns of lingonberry greens, bring trays of coffee and saffron sweet buns to their parents' beds. Christmas Eve is the most splendid celebration with a lavish candlelit *smörgåsbord* featuring a massive baked ham, *lutfisk* (a sun-dried, lime-cured fish), *risengrød* (a rice-porridge dessert) and plates of cookies and cakes. Feasting continues on December 25, 26, 27 and for many Scandinavians the holiday season does not end until Saint Canute's Day, January 13.

Flarn

These Swedish almond-lace rolled cookies are part of a lovely European tradition of very thin rolled wafers. They look spectacular on a plate of Christmas cookies.

⅔ cup	ground almonds	150 mL
½ cup	sugar	125 mL
½ cup	butter OR margarine	125 mL
2 tbsp.	milk	30 mL
1 tbsp.	flour	15 mL

Preheat oven to 350°F (180°C). In a heavy skillet, combine almonds, sugar, butter, milk and flour; stir over medium heat until butter melts. Drop teaspoonfuls of batter, 4" (10 cm) apart, on a well-greased and floured baking sheet, making about 6 cookies per sheet. Bake for 5-8 minutes, or until golden brown. Remove from oven. Let cool 1 minute; then, using a metal spatula, quickly and gently lift and place cookies over a rolling pin or roll around the handle of a wooden spoon. If cookies get too hard to roll, quickly reheat them in the oven. Let rolled cookies cool about 1 minute, or until curved and firm. Gently remove cookies from rolling pin and let cool on wire rack. Grease and flour the cookie sheets each time. Store cookies in airtight containers or freeze for up to 3 months.

Makes about 36 cookies

Variations:

 For an even more sumptuous presentation, fill the rolled cookies with flavored whipped cream or dip one or both ends in melted chocolate. You can also dip one end in white chocolate and one end in dark chocolate.

Orechove Kolieska Zlepovane

(Czechoslovakian Raspberry Walnut Sandwiches)

Sugar Biscuits:

1 cup	butter	250 mL
¾ cup	icing sugar	175 mL
1 tsp.	vanilla	5 mL
1	egg, lightly beaten	1
2½ cups	flour	625 mL

Walnut Rum Filling:

½ cup	icing sugar	125 mL
2 tbsp.	water	30 mL
1 cup	ground walnuts	250 mL
2 tbsp.	rum	30 mL
1 tsp.	vanilla	5 mL
⅓ cup	seedless raspberry jam	75 mL

Chocolate Glaze:

5 x 1 oz.	squares semisweet chocolate	5 x 30 g

To make the biscuits, in a large bowl, cream butter; beat in icing sugar and vanilla until light and fluffy. Gradually beat in egg; stir in flour, kneading with fingers to form soft dough. Divide dough in half; form each half into a ball. Wrap and chill for 30 minutes.

Preheat oven to 350°F (180°C). Between 2 sheets of waxed paper, roll out half of the dough to ⅛" (3 mm) thickness. With fluted 1½" (4 cm) cutter, cut dough into rounds. Arrange on ungreased baking sheet about ½" (1.3 cm) apart. Bake for 8-10 minutes, or until golden around edges. Let cool on wire rack. Repeat with remaining dough.

To make the filling, in a large bowl, gradually stir sugar into water until smooth. Add walnuts, rum and vanilla; mix well. Spread a small amount of raspberry jam on half of the biscuits. Add about ½ tsp. (2 mL) walnut filling to each and top with remaining biscuits.

Orechove Kolieska Zlepovane

Continued

To make the glaze, in a double boiler over hot (not boiling) water, melt chocolate, stirring constantly. Using a table knife or metal spatula, spread chocolate on top of sandwiched cookies. Let stand in a cool place or refrigerate until chocolate sets. Store in an airtight container for up to 1 week or wrap well and freeze for up to 3 months.

Makes about 60 cookies

Kourabiedes

(Greek Shortbread)

These icing sugar-coated shortbread crescents have a delicate almond flavor.

2 cups	butter, softened	500 mL
¾ cup	sugar	175 mL
2	egg yolks	2
1½ cups	finely ground toasted almonds	375 mL
5-6 cups	flour	1.25-1.5 L
	icing sugar	

Preheat oven to 350°F (180°C). Cream butter and sugar together until light and fluffy. Add egg yolks and toasted almonds. Stir in enough flour to make a soft dough. Squeeze the dough between your fingers for about 15 minutes. Break off bits of dough and roll into crescents. Place on ungreased cookie sheets. Bake for 20 minutes, or until pale brown in color. While still hot, dredge with icing sugar. Cool thoroughly on racks before storing. Store in airtight containers for 5 days or freeze for up to 3 months.

Makes about 84 cookies

Traditional Scottish Shortbread

Uncle Red, Jo's brother-in-law, one of the last of the Whistling Plow Boys, brought this crisp, buttery shortbread recipe from Scotland.

2 cups	butter	500 mL
1 cup	icing sugar	250 mL
3 cups	flour	750 mL
¾ cup	cornstarch	175 mL

Cream butter and add the sugar gradually. Blend well, but do not overwork it or let the butter become oily. Combine the flour and cornstarch and gradually work it into the butter mixture. Turn the dough out on a lightly floured (use half flour and half icing sugar) board to pat out. Pat the dough into 2 circles, about ¾" (2 cm) thick. Pinch the edges, and prick all over with a fork. Place on a baking sheet. Chill in refrigerator or freezer for half an hour. Preheat oven at 375°F (190°C). Bake shortbread at this temperature for 5 minutes, then lower temperature to 300°F (150°C) and continue baking for 45-60 minutes. When done, shortbread should be golden, but not browned at all. Cut into wedges while still warm. Store in airtight containers for 5 days or freeze for up to 3 months. Makes about 32 wedges.

Pictured on page 51.

Variations:

🍪🍪 **Shortbread Cookies**, instead of wedges, pat the dough out to ¼-½" (6-12 mm) thickness. Cut in small rounds with a cookie cutter. Prick each round twice with a fork, chill and bake, as above, for a total of 20 minutes. Makes about 75 cookies

🍪🍪 **Ginger Shortbread**, add ¾ cup (175 mL) chopped candied ginger.
🍪🍪 **Lemon Shortbread**, add 4 tbsp. (60 mL) grated lemon zest.
🍪🍪 **Whipped Shortbread**, put softened butter in a bowl, add icing sugar, a bit at a time; beat with an electric mixer. Beat in flour and cornstarch (increase cornstarch to 1 cup [250 mL]) a bit at a time. Beat for about 20 minutes, longer beating makes lighter shortbread. Drop batter from a small spoon onto ungreased cookie sheets or use a cookie press. Bake at 300°F (180°C) for 25-30 minutes. Makes about 70 cookies.

Brown Sugar Shortbread

Sherry McFarlane, a dear and loveable friend, graces our holiday festivities with this shortbread every year. Some years they are plain and some years she dresses them up with cherries or gumdrops. In any version they are gratefully received and the first to disappear from the cookie plate.

2 cups	butter	500 mL
1 cup	brown sugar	250 mL
¼-1 tsp.	vanilla	1-5 mL
4 cups	flour	1 L

Preheat oven to 350°F (180°C). Cream butter and sugar together thoroughly. Add vanilla and mix well. Add flour in 4 portions, mixing well after each addition. Turn onto a mixing board and knead until all cracks have disappeared. Spread dough evenly in an ungreased 9" (23 cm) square pan and prick deeply with a fork. Bake for 20-30 minutes. Cut into squares. Store in airtight containers for 5 days or freeze for up to 3 months.

Makes 36 squares

Pictured on page 51.

Variations:

For **Shortbread Wedges** use a small round cake pan and cut baked shortbread into wedges.

For **Shortbread Cookies**, roll dough into small balls, place on ungreased cookie sheets and press down with a floured fork. Add Christmas decorations if you wish – colored sugar sprinkles, silver dragées or a quarter of a candied cherry in the center of each cookie. Bake cookies for about 20 minutes.

Makes about 60 cookies

Almond Biscotti

These twice-baked Italian cookies are very hard and crisp, perfect for dunking into hot chocolate, coffee, tea or even wine.

1¾ cups	flour	425 mL
2 tsp.	baking powder	10 mL
¾ cup	whole unblanched almonds	175 mL
2	eggs	2
¾ cup	sugar	175 mL
⅓ cup	butter, melted	75 mL
2 tsp.	vanilla	10 mL
½ tsp.	almond extract	2 mL
1½ tsp.	grated orange rind	7 mL
1	egg white, lightly beaten	1

In a large bowl, combine flour, baking powder and almonds. In a separate bowl, whisk together eggs, sugar, melted butter, vanilla, almond extract and grated orange rind; stir into flour mixture until a soft, sticky dough forms. Transfer dough to a lightly floured work surface; with hands, form into a smooth ball. Preheat oven to 350°F (180°C). Divide dough in half; roll each half into a flattish 12" (30 cm) long log. Transfer to an ungreased baking sheet. Brush tops with egg white; bake for 20 minutes. Remove from oven and let cool on a pan or rack for 5 minutes. Transfer each log to a cutting board. With a very sharp knife, cut diagonally into ¾" (3 cm) thick slices. Stand cookies upright on a baking sheet; bake for 20-25 minutes longer, or until golden. Let cool on rack. Biscotti can be stored in airtight containers for up to 2 weeks.

Makes 24 cookies

Gift Suggestion: Pack Biscotti into tall glass jars for very elegant gifts. For an even more spectacular gift, dip Biscotti tips into melted white or dark chocolate.

Yule Love It

(Christmas Baking)

Mom's Steamed Carrot Christmas Pudding, page 27
Caramel Sauce, page 28
Holiday Sugar Cookies, page 40
Mom's Traditional Christmas Cake, page 35
Dark Fruit Cake, page 34
Traditional Scottish Shortbread, page 48
Brown Sugar Shortbread, page 49

Mexican Mocha Balls

A hint of coffee adds a unique flavor to this holiday cookie.

1 cup	butter, softened	250 mL
½ cup	sugar	125 mL
1 tsp.	vanilla	5 mL
¼ cup	cocoa	60 mL
1 tsp.	instant coffee	5 mL
¼ tsp.	salt	1 mL
2 cups	flour	500 mL
½ cup	finely chopped maraschino cherries	125 mL
½ cup	finely chopped walnuts OR pecans	125 mL
	sugar to coat cookies	

In a bowl, beat butter with sugar until light and fluffy; beat in vanilla. Beat in cocoa, coffee and salt; stir in flour until well combined. Add cherries and walnuts. Cover dough and refrigerate for 1 hour. Preheat oven to 325°F (160°C). Form dough into 1" (2.5 cm) balls; roll in sugar to coat lightly. Bake on ungreased baking sheets for 20 minutes, or until top starts to crack. Remove from oven and place on a wire rack to cool. Store in airtight containers for up to 5 days or freeze.

Makes about 40 cookies

Variation:

If desired, drizzle melted chocolate over cooled balls.

🕯 Mexican Christmas Traditions 🕯

Children in Mexico carry lighted candles during processions called *posadas* from December 16 to Christmas Eve. They are searching for an inn to shelter Mary and Joseph. Each evening, when they find the *posada* or inn, there is feasting and fireworks. *Piñatas*, decorated clay jars in bird or animal shapes and filled with small presents and candies, are hung up and blindfolded children take turns hitting them with sticks until they break and the treats spill out. The final *posada*, on Christmas Eve, is followed by midnight mass to celebrate the birth of Jesus. Fireworks and ringing church bells follow the prayers. Presents are given on the feast of the Three Kings, January 6.

Angel Pillows

The delicate apricot flavor makes these a wonderful addition to any holiday tray.

½ cup	golden-flavored shortening	125 mL
4 oz.	cream cheese, softened	125 g
¼ cup	milk	60 mL
¼ cup	brown sugar	60 mL
¾ cup	apricot jam	175 mL
1¼ cups	flour	300 mL
2 tsp.	baking powder	10 mL
1½ tsp.	cinnamon	7 mL
¼ tsp.	salt	1 mL
½ cup	finely chopped pecans OR flaked coconut	125 mL

Apricot Frosting:

1 cup	icing sugar	250 mL
¼ cup	apricot jam	60 mL
1 tbsp.	golden-flavored shortening	15 mL
	chopped pecans OR flaked coconut	

Preheat oven to 350°F (180°C). Combine shortening, cream cheese, milk, brown sugar and jam in a large bowl. With an electric mixer, at medium speed, beat until well blended. Combine flour, baking powder, cinnamon and salt. Add to creamed mixture, beating at low speed until smooth. Stir in nuts or coconut. Drop dough by heaping spoonfuls onto a greased baking sheet. Bake for 12-15 minutes, or until light gold. Remove from oven and cool completely.

To make Apricot Frosting, combine icing sugar, jam and shortening, stirring until smooth. Spread over cooled cookies. Sprinkle with chopped pecans or coconut. Store in airtight containers and freeze for up to 3 months.

Makes 24 cookies

Dapper Cookies

*This moist chewy cookie full of fruit, cereal and nuts
has wonderful texture and flavor.*

1 cup	butter OR margarine	250 mL
1 cup	white sugar	250 mL
1 cup	brown sugar	250 mL
2	eggs	2
2 tsp.	vanilla	10 mL
2 cups	flour	500 mL
1 tsp.	baking soda	5 mL
1 tsp.	baking powder	5 mL
1 tsp.	salt	5 mL
2 cups	rolled oats	500 mL
2 cups	slightly crushed cornflakes	500 mL
1 cup	coconut	250 mL
1 cup	raisins	250 mL
1 cup	chopped candied cherries	250 mL
1 cup	chopped walnuts	250 mL

Preheat oven to 375°F (190°C). Cream butter and sugars together. Add eggs and vanilla and beat until light and fluffy. Combine flour, baking soda, baking powder and salt and add to butter mixture. Blend well. Add rolled oats and cornflakes; blend well. Add fruit and nuts and blend well. Drop by small spoonfuls onto a greased cookie sheet. Bake for 10-12 minutes. Store in airtight containers and freeze for up to 3 months.

Makes approximately 60 cookies

The Poinsettia

A Mexican legend tells about a poor boy and his sister who were sadly watching people carry gifts for the Christ Child into the church on Christmas Eve. Near the church was a stone angel, behind some weeds. The children heard the angel tell them to gather the weeds and take them into the church as a gift. When laid by the Christ Child's manger the leaves at the top of each stem turned into a flaming red. Poinsettias are some-times called Fire Flowers of the Holy Night.

Mom Mandryk's Christmas Nuggets

Fruit-filled moist morsels, these cookies develop flavor over 2-3 days.
They are great make-aheads.

2 cups	chopped dates	500 mL
½ cup	hot water	125 mL
1 tsp.	baking soda	5 mL
1 cup	butter OR margarine	250 mL
1½ cups	brown sugar	375 mL
2	eggs	2
¼ cup	molasses	60 mL
2 tsp.	maple flavoring	10 mL
3½ cups	flour	875 mL
1 tsp.	baking powder	5 mL
1 tsp.	ground allspice	5 mL
1 tsp.	ground cloves	5 mL
1 tsp.	cinnamon	5 mL
1 cup	mixed candied fruit	250 mL
½ cup	chopped cherries	125 mL
1 cup	raisins	250 mL
1 cup	chopped walnuts	250 mL

Place dates in a bowl and pour the hot water over; add baking soda and let stand for about 15 minutes to soften dates. Preheat oven to 375°F (190°C). Cream butter and sugar until light and fluffy. Add eggs, molasses and maple flavoring; beat well. Stir in the date mixture and combine well. Combine the flour, baking powder, allspice, cloves and cinnamon and add to the date mixture. Add fruit and nuts and combine well. Drop by small spoonfuls onto a greased cookie sheet. Bake for 10-15 minutes. Cool and pack into containers. They should mature in the refrigerator for 2-3 days, then freeze for up to 3 months.

Makes approximately 60 cookies

Chocolate-Covered Cherry Cookies

These are wonderful – wonderful – wonderful, cherries smothered in chocolate icing on a chewy brownie base.

1½ cups	flour	375 mL
½ cup	cocoa	125 mL
¼ tsp.	salt	1 mL
¼ tsp.	baking powder	1 mL
¼ tsp.	baking soda	1 mL
½ cup	butter OR margarine, softened	125 mL
1 cup	sugar	250 mL
1	egg	1
1½ tsp.	vanilla	7 mL
10 oz.	jar maraschino cherries (about 48)	284 mL
1 cup	semisweet chocolate chips	250 mL
½ cup	sweetened condensed milk	125 mL

Preheat oven to 350°F (180°C). In a large bowl stir together flour, cocoa, salt, baking powder and baking soda. In a mixing bowl beat together, butter and sugar on low speed with an electric mixer, until fluffy. Add egg and vanilla; beat well. Gradually add dry ingredients to creamed mixture; beat until well blended. Shape dough in 1" (2.5 cm) balls; place on ungreased cookie sheet. Press down center of dough with thumb. Drain maraschino cherries, reserving juice. Place a cherry in the center of each cookie. In small saucepan combine chocolate chips and sweetened condensed milk; heat until chocolate is melted. Stir in 4 tsp. (20 mL) of the reserved cherry juice. Spoon about 1 tsp. (5 mL) of the frosting over each cookie, spreading to cover the cherry. (Frosting may be thinned with additional cherry juice, if necessary.) Bake about 10 minutes, or until done. Remove to wire rack; cool. Store in airtight containers and freeze for up to 3 months.

Makes about 48 cookies

Holiday Hideaways

Succulent cherries are baked in a cookie layer and then coated with chocolate and pecans – a tantalizing holiday treat.

⅔ cup	golden-flavored shortening	150 mL
¾ cup	sugar	175 mL
1	egg	1
1 tsp.	vanilla	5 mL
½ tsp.	almond extract	2 mL
1¾ cups	flour	425 mL
1 tsp.	baking powder	5 mL
½ tsp.	salt	2 mL
48	maraschino cherries, well drained and patted dry	48

Chocolate Coating:

6-8 x 1 oz.	squares semisweet chocolate	6-8 x 30 g
3 tbsp.	golden-flavored shortening	45 mL
	finely chopped pecans	

Preheat oven to 350°F (180°C). In a large bowl combine shortening, sugar, egg, vanilla and almond extract. With electric mixer at medium speed, beat until well blended. Combine flour, baking powder and salt. Add to creamed mixture, beating at low speed until smooth. Wrap dough around cherries in a very thin layer. Place cherries on an ungreased baking sheet. Bake for 10-12 minutes. Cool completely.

To make coating, melt chocolate and shortening together, stirring until smooth. Dip cooled cookies in chocolate, 1 at a time, turning to coat completely. Lift cookie out of chocolate on a fork and let excess drip off. Place on waxed paper-lined baking sheet. Sprinkle chopped pecans on top of cookies while chocolate is still wet. Chill to set chocolate. Store in airtight containers and freeze for up to 3 months.

Makes 48 cookies

Variation:

Cookies can also be rolled in icing sugar instead of chocolate. If using icing sugar, roll cookies while still warm.

Chocolate Pecan Bars

This chewy nut bar has a shortbread base and a rich chewy filling.

Shortbread Base:

2 cups	flour	500 mL
⅓ cup	sugar	75 mL
⅔ cup	butter OR margarine, softened	150 mL

Chocolate Pecan Filling:

6 x 1 oz.	squares semisweet chocolate	6 x 30 g
1½ cups	corn syrup	375 mL
1½ cups	sugar	375 mL
4	eggs, slightly beaten	4
1½ tsp.	vanilla	7 mL
2¼ cups	chopped pecans	625 mL

Chocolate Topping:

2 x 1 oz.	squares semisweet chocolate	2 x 30 g

Preheat oven to 350°F (180°C). For the crust, combine flour, sugar and butter in a large bowl. Beat on medium speed with electric mixer until mixture resembles coarse crumbs. Press firmly and evenly into a greased 10 x 15" (25 x 38 cm) jelly-roll pan. Bake for 15 minutes.

For the filling, heat chocolate and corn syrup in a saucepan over low heat, stirring until smoothly melted. Remove from heat. Stir in sugar, eggs and vanilla until blended. Stir in pecans. Pour filling over hot crust; spread evenly. Bake for 25-30 minutes, or until filling is firm around edges and slightly soft in center. Cool in pan on rack.

For the topping, melt chocolate over hot water or in microwave on medium for 2-3 minutes. Drizzle chocolate over the cooled bars. Cool and cut into squares. These freeze well.

Makes 60 bars

Rocky Road Fudge Bars

*This rich triple-chocolate bar may take a little time to prepare,
but is well worth the effort.*

Fudge Layer:

2 x 1 oz.	squares unsweetened chocolate	2 x 30 g
½ cup	butter OR margarine	125 mL
1 cup	sugar	250 mL
2	eggs	2
1 tsp.	vanilla	5 mL
1 cup	flour	250 mL
1 tsp.	baking powder	5 mL
½ cup	chopped walnuts OR pecans	125 mL

Chocolate Cream Cheese Layer:

¼ cup	butter OR margarine	60 mL
6 oz.	cream cheese, softened (from an 8 oz. [250 g] pkg.)	195 g
½ cup	sugar	125 mL
1	egg	1
2 tbsp.	flour	30 mL
½ tsp.	vanilla	2 mL
1 cup	semisweet chocolate chips	250 mL
¼ cup	chopped walnuts OR pecans	60 mL
⅔ cup	miniature marshmallows	150 mL

Creamy Chocolate Frosting:

¼ cup	butter OR margarine	60 mL
2 oz.	cream cheese, softened	65 g
2 x 1 oz.	squares unsweetened chocolate	2 x 30 g
3 tbsp.	milk	45 mL
3 cups	icing sugar	750 mL
1 tsp.	vanilla	5 mL

To prepare fudge layer, combine chocolate and butter in saucepan.
Cook over low heat until both are melted. Remove from heat. Stir in
sugar, eggs, vanilla, flour, baking powder and nuts. Mix well to combine. Spread mixture in the bottom of a greased 9 x 13" (23 x 33 cm)
baking pan and set aside.

Rocky Road Fudge Bars

Continued

Preheat oven to 350°F (180°C). To prepare cheese layer, beat together butter and cream cheese in a large bowl until light in texture. Stir in sugar, egg, flour, vanilla, chocolate chips and nuts. Mix until well combined. Spread over the fudge layer and bake for 25-30 minutes, or until set.

Prepare frosting while bars are baking. Combine butter, cream cheese, chocolate and milk in saucepan. Cook over low heat until mixture is melted. (Mixture may appear curdled at this point.) Remove from heat; stir in icing sugar and vanilla. If mixture is too thick to spread, add a little milk.

Remove bars from oven, sprinkle with marshmallows and return to oven for 2 minutes longer. Remove bars from oven. Immediately pour frosting over top and swirl marshmallows and frosting together. Cool in pan on wire rack until firm. Cut into squares. These freeze well.

Makes 48 bars

✎ The First Christmas Crackers ✎

No Christmas party in Britain is complete without a box of "crackers".

Christmas crackers were first made in Britain about 70 years ago. It was a confectioner and maker of ornaments for wedding cakes with the typical English name of Tom Smith who brought back from a holiday on the Continent the idea which evolved into the cracker. He saw that a French confectioner made his sweetmeats more attractive by wrapping them in tissue paper. A few weeks before Christmas he set his assistant wrapping sugared almonds in this way. The cracker of today came a little nearer when he thought of making the package more entertaining by placing a loving message inside. Christmas crackers today usually contain colorful paper hats, small toys and riddles or jokes.

Turtle Bars

The combined flavors of chocolate, caramel and pecans are sinfully delicious. This "instant" version is very easy to make.

19 oz.	dark chocolate cake mix, 2-layer size and other ingredients called for on cake box	520 g
1 cup	butter OR margarine	250 mL
1 cup	brown sugar, packed	250 mL
¼ cup	corn syrup	60 mL
1 cup	sweetened condensed milk	250 mL
2 cups	chopped pecans	500 mL
1 cup	semisweet chocolate chips	250 mL

Preheat oven to 350°F (180°C). Prepare cake mix according to package directions. Divide batter in half. Pour half into a greased 9 x 13" (23 x 33 cm) pan. Set other half of batter aside. Bake batter in pan for 15 minutes. Meanwhile, put butter, sugar, syrup and milk into a heavy saucepan. Heat and stir over medium heat until it boils. Boil for 5 minutes, stirring constantly as it burns easily. Pour over baked cake. Sprinkle with 1 cup (250 mL) pecans and chocolate chips. Pour second half of batter over top. Sprinkle batter with the remaining chopped pecans. Bake for 25-30 minutes more. Cool and cut into bars. Store in an airtight container. These freeze well.

Makes 48 bars

Silent Night

Austrian Carol

Silent night, Holy night,
All is calm, all is bright;
Round yon virgin mother and child,
Holy infant so tender and mild,
Sleep in heavenly peace,
Sleep in heavenly peace.

Silent night, Holy night,
Shepherds quake at the sight;
Glories stream from heaven afar,
Heav'nly hosts sing Alleluia!
Christ the Saviour is born!
Christ the Saviour is born!

Silent night, Holy night
Son of God, love's pure light;
Radiance beams from Thy holy face,
With the dawn of redeeming grace,
Jesus, Lord at Thy birth,
Jesus, Lord at Thy birth.

Shortbread Caramel Fingers

Rich caramel on a shortbread base topped with chocolate – these are also called Millionaires' Shortbread because they are so luxurious.

Shortbread Base:

1 cup	butter OR margarine	250 mL
2 cups	flour	500 mL
½ cup	berry sugar	125 mL
⅛ tsp.	salt	0.5 mL

Caramel Filling:

10 oz.	can sweetened condensed milk	300 mL
1 cup	brown sugar	250 mL
1 cup	butter OR margarine	250 mL
4 tbsp.	corn syrup	60 mL
2 cups	semisweet chocolate chips	500 mL

Preheat oven to 350°F (180°C). To make base, combine butter, flour, berry sugar and salt in a bowl. Crumble together well. Press into 2, 9" (23 cm) square pans or into a 10 x 15" (25 x 38 cm) jelly-roll pan. Bake for 25 minutes.

To make the caramel filling, in a saucepan, combine the sweetened condensed milk, brown sugar, butter and corn syrup. Stirring constantly over medium-low heat, bring milk mixture to a boil and boil for 7 minutes. Remember to stir constantly as it will burn very easily when boiling. Remove from heat and beat with a spoon for about 1 minute. Pour the caramel over the shortbread base. Melt the chocolate chips and pour over the caramel layer. Mark and cut before the chocolate hardens. These freeze well.

Makes 60 squares

Caramel Bars

A caramel lover's delight.

1 cup	flour	250 mL
1 cup	rolled oats	250 mL
½ tsp.	baking soda	2 mL
¼ tsp.	salt	1 mL
¾ cup	butter OR margarine	175 mL
¾ cup	sugar	175 mL
14 oz.	pkg. caramels	400 g
⅓ cup	evaporated milk	75 mL
½ cup	chopped walnuts OR pecans	125 mL
1 cup	butterscotch chips OR semisweet chocolate chips	250 mL

Preheat oven to 350°F (180°C). Combine flour, oats, baking soda and salt. In a mixing bowl beat butter 30 seconds with an electric mixer. Add sugar; beat until fluffy. Beat in oat mixture just until crumbly. Reserve 1 cup (250 mL) of base mixture; press remaining mixture into bottom of a 9 x 13" (23 x 33 cm) baking pan. Bake for 10 minutes. Cool in pan 10 minutes. Meanwhile, in a saucepan over low heat stir caramels and evaporated milk until caramels melt and mixture is smooth. Spread over baked crust. Sprinkle with nuts, reserved crumbs and chips. Bake for an additional 15-20 minutes, or until topping is golden. Cool in pan on rack. Cut into bars. These freeze well.

Makes 48

⚫ *Austrian Christmas Traditions* ⚫

Christmas is celebrated by people in Austria with the baking of two loaves of bread. One stands for the Old Testament and one stands for the New.

Almond Bars

This is a chewy, buttery, nutty bar.

Brown Sugar Base:

½ cup	butter OR margarine, melted	125 mL
2 cups	brown sugar	500 mL
2	eggs	2
1½ tsp.	vanilla	7 mL
1½ cups	flour	375 mL
2 tsp.	baking powder	10 mL

Almond Filling:

¼ cup	butter OR margarine	60 mL
⅓ cup	sugar	75 mL
⅓ cup	corn syrup	75 mL
2 tbsp.	water	30 mL
¼ tsp.	salt	1 mL
1½ cups	sliced almonds	375 mL

Chocolate Topping:

½ cup	semisweet chocolate chips	125 mL

Preheat oven to 325°F (160°C). For the base, combine melted butter with the brown sugar. Add eggs and vanilla and mix well. Combine flour and baking powder and add to the butter mixture. Mix well and spread evenly in a 9 x 13" (23 x 33 cm) baking pan. Bake for 20 minutes.

Meanwhile, in a saucepan, prepare the filling. Combine butter, sugar, corn syrup, water and salt. Over medium-low heat, bring this to a boil and boil for 4 minutes, stirring constantly. Remove from heat and stir in the sliced almonds. Spread almond filling evenly over the warm base and return to the oven. Bake 10-15 minutes. Cool on a rack.

Melt chocolate chips and drizzle over the top once the bars are cool. Cut into squares. These freeze well.

Makes 48 bars

Lemon Squares

The tangy flavor of lemon is mouthwatering on a shortbread crust.

Shortbread Base:

1 cup	flour	250 mL
¼ cup	icing sugar	60 mL
½ cup	butter OR margarine	125 mL

Lemon Layer:

2 tbsp.	flour	30 mL
1 cup	sugar	250 mL
2	eggs, lightly beaten	2
2 tbsp.	lemon juice	30 mL
2 tsp.	grated lemon peel	10 mL

Preheat oven to 350°F (180°C). To make the base, combine flour, icing sugar and butter. Mix until crumbly. Press into an 8" (20 cm) square pan and bake for 20 minutes. Cool.

To make the lemon layer, combine the flour and sugar. Mix the lightly beaten eggs, lemon juice and rind and add to the sugar-flour mixture. Mix well. Pour over the baked crust and bake an additional 25 minutes. Cool on wire rack. Cut into squares. These freeze well.

Makes 24 bars

 ## The Christmas Crèche

In Italy, St. Francis of Assisi, the patron saint of animals, set up the first manger scene, life-sized, with real animals and villagers playing the parts of Mary, Joseph and the shepherds. The custom spread across Europe and miniature manger scenes were created. In France the children often set up the small figures and decide where to place the crèche. *Le Petit Noël*, the Christ Child, is usually placed in the manger on Christmas Eve.

Coconut Almond Tarts

3	eggs, beaten	3
1 cup	medium unsweetened coconut	250 mL
1 cup	sugar	250 mL
3½ oz.	pkg. slivered almonds	100 g
¼ cup	flour	60 mL
½ cup	milk	125 mL
1 tsp.	almond extract	5 mL
24	unbaked tart shells	24

Preheat oven to 350°F (180°C). In a medium bowl, beat eggs and add all remaining ingredients, except for tart shells. Place about 2 tbsp. (30 mL) of filling in each shell or fill shells ¾ full. Bake for 25-30 minutes, or until golden brown. These freeze well.

Makes 24 tarts

Variation:

 For added flavor, place 1 tsp. (5 mL) of raspberry jam or jelly at the bottom of each tart shell before spooning in the coconut filling.

Merry Christmas Around the World

Bohemia – *Vesele Vanoce*
Bulgaria – *Chestita Koleda*
Croatia – *Sretan Bojic*
Denmark – *Gledelig Jul!*
England – *Happy Christmas!*
Finland – *Hauskaa Joulua!*
France – *Joyeux Noël!*
Germany – *Froehliche Weihnachten*
Greece – *Eftihismena Christougenna!*
Ireland – *Nodlaig Mhaith Chugnat*

Italy – *Buon Natale!*
Netherlands – *Prettige Kerstdagen*
Norway – *Glaedelig Jul!*
Poland – *Weselych Swiat*
Portugal & Brazil – *Boas Festas*
Russia – *Hristos Razdajetsja!*
Spain & Mexico – *¡Felices Pascuas*
Sweden – *Gud Jul!*
Ukraine – *Khrystos Razdayetsia*
Wales – *Nadolig Llawen*

Mom's Butter Tarts

2	eggs, well beaten	2
2 cups	brown sugar	500 mL
2 tbsp.	vinegar	30 mL
1 tsp.	vanilla	5 mL
½ cup	melted butter	125 mL
1⅓ cups	currants and raisins	325 mL
	chopped nuts (optional)	
24	tart shells, see Mom's Pastry, below	24

Preheat oven to 400°F (200°C). In a medium bowl, beat eggs then combine all ingredients, except for tart shells. Mix well. Fill each shell about ¾ full. Bake for 15-20 minutes. These freeze well.

Mom's Pastry

Mom's secret to flaky pastry is a light touch; "Do Not Overwork Pastry".

1 lb.	lard	500 g
5-5½ cups	flour	1.25-1.375 L
½ tsp.	salt	2 mL
1	egg, beaten	1
2 tbsp.	vinegar	30 mL
¾ cup	ice-cold water	175 mL

Cut lard into flour and salt. In a 1 cup (250 mL) measure, beat egg with fork. Add vinegar and enough cold water to make 1 cup (250 mL). Stir egg mixture into flour mixture. Add the ice water and mix well. Wrap in waxed paper and chill or freeze before using. Roll out as required for tarts, pies, etc.

Why Not Brunch?

Brunch Dishes
Breads
Muffins

Caramel Oven French Toast

This easy to prepare "make-ahead" dish will be a hit on Christmas morning or for special brunches year round.

1	loaf French bread, cut in 1" (2.5 cm) slices	1
8	large eggs	8
2 cups	milk	500 mL
2 cups	half and half cereal cream	500 mL
2 tsp.	vanilla	10 mL
½ tsp.	cinnamon	2 mL

Caramel Topping:

¾ cup	butter OR margarine	175 mL
1½ cups	brown sugar	375 mL
3 tbsp.	dark corn syrup	45 mL
1½ cups	chopped nuts	375 mL

Grease a 9 x 13" (23 x 33 cm) pan. Fill the pan with bread slices to ½" (1.3 cm) from top. Set aside. In a large mixing bowl, using an electric mixer, beat eggs, milk, cereal cream, vanilla and cinnamon. Beat well for 2-3 minutes. Pour the mixture over the bread slices. Refrigerate, covered, overnight.

Preheat oven to 350°F (180°C). To make topping, melt butter in a saucepan over very low heat, add the brown sugar and corn syrup. Heat, stirring constantly, until mixture is smoothly combined. Remove from heat and add nuts. Set aside until time to bake toast, then spread topping over toast. Bake for 50 minutes, until puffed and golden. If top browns too quickly, shield with foil.

Serves 8-10

Pictured on page 85.

Puffed Apple Pancakes

*Pancakes with a different twist, these are baked in the oven
and have a fabulous apple cinnamon flavor.*

6	eggs	6
1½ cups	milk	375 mL
1 cup	flour	250 mL
3 tbsp.	granulated sugar	45 mL
1 tsp.	vanilla	5 mL
½ tsp.	salt	2 mL
¼ tsp.	cinnamon	1 mL
½ cup	butter OR margarine	125 mL
2	apples, peeled and thinly sliced	2
3 tbsp.	brown sugar	45 mL

Preheat oven to 425°F (220°C). In a blender or large bowl, mix eggs, milk, flour, 3 tbsp. (45 mL) granulated sugar, vanilla, salt and cinnamon until blended. If using an electric mixer, batter will remain slightly lumpy. Melt butter in a 9 x 13" (23 x 33 cm) baking dish in oven. Add apple slices to baking dish. Return to oven until butter sizzles. Do not let brown. Remove dish from oven and immediately pour batter over apples. Sprinkle with brown sugar. Bake in the middle of the oven for 20 minutes, or until puffed and brown. Serve immediately.

Makes 6-8 servings

🧦 Christmas Traditions 🧦

In Puerto Rico, instead of hanging up stockings to be filled on Christmas Eve, children put boxes on the roof. In Puerto Rico, Mexico and Spain, on January 6, the Three Kings bring gifts so children put hay in their shoes to feed the Kings' camels and they put their shoes on the window sills. In the Netherlands and Belgium, children put out *sabots* (wooden shoes) for the Christ Child to fill with gifts. In some countries, children put out baskets or plates to be filled with candies and gifts.

Pineapple Pancakes

Fantastic – buttermilk pancakes with a creamy pineapple sauce – try them.

Fluffy Buttermilk Pancakes:

3	eggs, separated	3
1⅔ cups	buttermilk	400 mL
1 tsp.	baking soda	5 mL
1½ cups	flour	375 mL
1 tbsp.	sugar	15 mL
1 tsp.	baking powder	5 mL
½ tsp.	salt	2 mL
3 tbsp.	soft butter	45 mL

Pineapple Sauce:

19 oz.	can crushed pineapple	540 mL
8 oz.	cream cheese, softened	250 g
2 tbsp.	half and half cereal cream	30 mL
2 tbsp.	sugar	30 mL
1½ tbsp.	cornstarch	22 mL

Beat egg yolks thoroughly. Beat in buttermilk and baking soda. Combine flour, sugar, baking powder and salt and add to buttermilk mixture. Beat to blend well. Beat in butter. In a separate bowl, beat egg whites until stiff and fold into batter. Drop batter by rounded table-spoonfuls on a lightly greased, medium hot griddle, spreading the batter slightly so finished cakes will measure about 2½" (6 cm) in diameter. Brown on first side and turn or flip carefully to lightly brown the second side. Keep warm in oven until all are cooked.

To prepare sauce, drain pineapple very well, pressing gently with a spoon to get out all excess juice. Save the juice. Beat cheese, cream and sugar until fluffy. Fold in well-drained pineapple. Set aside.

Measure juice from pineapple and add enough water to make 1½ cups (375 mL) of liquid. Combine ¼ cup (60 mL) of this liquid with cornstarch, stirring until smooth. Heat remaining liquid to boiling and stir in cornstarch mixture gradually. Boil until thick and clear, stirring constantly. Turn down heat and cook, stirring constantly, for 1 minute. Keep hot.

Pineapple Pancakes

Continued

To serve, place a pancake on an individual plate, spread 1-2 tsp. (5-10 mL) of pineapple cheese mixture on top. Top with another pancake. Again spread pineapple cheese mixture on top, then top with the pineapple syrup. To make larger servings, add a third pancake and additional topping before pouring on the syrup.

Serves 8

Potato Pancakes

These are fussy to make, but well worth the effort. The sour cream, bacon and onion flavors of the sauce are perfect with the crispy potato pancakes.

Sour Cream-Bacon Sauce:

1 cup	cooked and crumbled bacon	250 mL
¼ cup	chopped green onions	60 mL
2 cups	sour cream	500 mL

Potato Pancakes:

3	medium raw potatoes, pared	3
2	eggs	2
2 tbsp.	flour	30 mL
⅓ cup	minced onion	75 mL
½ tsp.	salt	2 mL
¼ tsp.	pepper	1 mL
	oil for frying	

To make the sauce, cook bacon crisp and crumble; chop onion and add both to sour cream. Combine well and set aside. Shred or grate potatoes and squeeze out excess moisture. In a mixing bowl, blend the eggs, potatoes and flour. Add the onion, salt and pepper. Combine well. Heat 2-3 tbsp. (30-45 mL) oil in a large skillet over medium-high heat. Drop the batter into the hot oil by large spoonfuls. Flatten slightly. Fry each side crisp and brown. Serve with sauce.

Makes 8 servings

Mexican Crêpes

Tantalize your taste buds with this tangy, "make-ahead" Mexican dish.

Crêpes:

2	eggs	2
2 cups	flour	500 mL
1 tsp.	salt	5 mL
1 tsp.	sugar	5 mL
¾-1 cup	milk	175-250 mL

Peppery Mexican Filling:

1 tbsp.	vegetable oil	15 mL
1	sweet green pepper, chopped	1
1	onion, chopped	1
1 cup	sliced mushrooms	250 mL
1 cup	tomato sauce	250 mL
	salt and pepper to taste	
6-8 drops	hot pepper sauce	6-8 drops
24 slices	mozzarella cheese	24 slices
	extra hot pepper sauce	

Sour Cream Topping:

1 cup	sour cream	250 mL
½ cup	shredded mozzarella cheese	125 mL

In a large bowl, beat eggs lightly. Combine flour, salt and sugar and add to eggs. Beat in enough milk to make a thin batter. Grease crêpe pan or 6-7" (15-18 cm) skillet lightly and heat over medium-high heat. Pour in about 2 tbsp. (30 mL) of batter. Fry crêpes on both sides and roll up immediately. Continue until all batter is used. Cover crêpes and set aside while preparing filling.

To make the filling, in a skillet over medium heat, heat oil and sauté the green pepper, onion and mushrooms until just tender. Remove from heat and add the tomato sauce, salt and pepper and hot pepper sauce. Stir well to combine.

Mexican Crêpes

Continued

Preheat oven to 325°F (160°C). To assemble crêpes, unroll each one and place on it a slice of cheese, 2 tsp. (10 mL) of the filling and a dash of hot pepper sauce. Roll up and place in a well-greased shallow casserole. Continue until all crêpes are used. Top with the sour cream and shredded mozzarella cheese. Cover and bake for 30-45 minutes. These can be made ahead and refrigerated for up to 2 days or frozen for up to 2 months.

Serves 8-10

Dilled Cheesy Hash Browns

A crowd pleaser, serve these anytime.

2 lbs.	frozen hash brown potatoes	1 kg
2 cups	plain yogurt OR sour cream	500 mL
10 oz.	can sliced mushrooms, drained	284 mL
¼ cup	chopped fresh dill OR 2 tbsp. (30 mL) dillweed	60 mL
2 x 10 oz.	cream of mushroom soup	2 x 284 mL
½ cup	melted butter OR margarine	125 mL
⅓ cup	chopped onion	75 mL
2 cups	grated Cheddar cheese	500 mL
	salt and pepper to taste	
¼-⅓ cup	grated Parmesan cheese	60-75 mL

Preheat oven to 350°F (180°C). Thaw potatoes slightly for easier mixing. In a large bowl, combine all ingredients except Parmesan cheese. Mix well. Pour potato mixture into a well-greased 9 x 13" (23 x 33 cm) baking dish. Sprinkle with Parmesan cheese. Bake for 1-1½ hours.

Serves 10-12

Holiday Brunch Pie

This easy-to-prepare omelet is baked on a bed of seasoned hash browns.

6	slices bacon, cooked and crumbled	6
3 tbsp.	butter OR margarine	45 mL
2 cups	frozen hash brown potatoes	500 mL
½ tsp.	celery salt	2 mL
¾ cup	sliced fresh mushrooms	175 mL
½ cup	chopped onion	125 mL
½ cup	chopped green pepper	125 mL
5	eggs	5
½ cup	milk	125 mL
⅛ tsp.	pepper	0.5 mL
1 cup	shredded Cheddar cheese	250 mL

Preheat oven to 325°F (160°C). Cook bacon and crumble. In a skillet over medium-high heat, melt butter. Sauté hash brown potatoes until browned and crusty, about 5 minutes. Sprinkle with celery salt and mix well. Spread evenly in a 9" (23 cm) quiche dish or pie plate. Top with mushrooms, onions and green pepper. Whisk together eggs, milk and pepper. Pour over potatoes in pan. Bake for 30 minutes, or until set. Remove from oven, and immediately sprinkle with cheese and crumbled bacon.

Makes 6 servings

Quiche Lorraine

A traditional dish that is popular any time of the year for brunch or lunch.

½ lb.	bacon, cooked and crumbled	250 g
9-10"	pastry-lined quiche dish OR pie plate	23-25 cm
1½ cups	shredded Swiss cheese	375 mL
4	eggs	4
2 cups	half and half cereal cream	500 mL
½ tsp.	salt	2 mL
	dash of freshly ground, black pepper	
	pinch of nutmeg (optional)	

Quiche Lorraine

Continued

Preheat oven to 375°F (190°C). Fry bacon until crisp. Crumble and distribute evenly over the bottom of the pie crust. Sprinkle shredded cheese over bacon. In a medium bowl, with electric beater, beat eggs with cream, salt, pepper and nutmeg until well blended but not frothy. Pour over bacon and cheese. Bake for 40 minutes, or until set, when a knife inserted in the middle comes out clean. Let sit for 10 minutes before serving.

Serves 6-8

Crustless Crab Quiche

This cheesy, mild-flavored, easy-to-prepare dish is great when you want an alternative to pie crust.

2 tbsp.	butter OR margarine	30 mL
1 cup	thinly sliced mushrooms	250 mL
1	small onion, finely chopped	1
4	eggs	4
1 cup	cottage cheese	250 mL
1 cup	sour cream	250 mL
¼ cup	flour	60 mL
¼ tsp.	salt	1 mL
½ cup	grated Parmesan cheese	125 mL
1 cup	grated Cheddar cheese	250 mL
6 oz.	can crab meat, drained	184 g

Preheat oven to 350°F (180°C). Heat butter and sauté mushrooms and onion until tender. Set aside. In a blender or food processor place all other ingredients except the Cheddar cheese and crab meat. Blend until thoroughly mixed. Pour into a mixing bowl and fold in sautéed mushrooms and onions, the Cheddar cheese and crab meat. Pour into a greased 9-10" (23 x 25 cm) quiche dish or pie plate. Bake for 45 minutes, or until set, when a knife inserted in the middle comes out clean. Let sit for 10 minutes before serving.

Serves 6-8

Pictured on page 85.

Fantastic Mushroom Three-Cheese Eggs

This sensational cheesy egg dish is guaranteed to win accolades.

2 tbsp.	butter	30 mL
1 lb.	fresh mushrooms, thinly sliced	500 g
	dash of salt and pepper	
12	eggs	12
½ cup	butter	125 mL

Cream Sauce:

6 tbsp.	butter	90 mL
6 tbsp.	flour	90 mL
dash	salt and pepper	dash
2 cups	half and half cereal cream	500 mL
1 cup	grated Parmesan cheese	250 mL
1 cup	grated Swiss OR Gruyère cheese	250 mL
1 cup	grated Cheddar cheese	250 mL

Melt 2 tbsp. (30 mL) of butter in a large skillet over medium heat. Sauté mushrooms until soft. Add salt and pepper. Set aside. In a large bowl whisk eggs thoroughly. Add salt and pepper. Melt half of the ½ cup (125 mL) butter in a large skillet over very low heat; add eggs and gently scramble to very soft curd stage. Stir in remaining butter and sprinkle with salt and pepper. Set aside. To make the sauce, melt butter in a saucepan at medium low. Stir in flour. Add salt and pepper. Stir in half and half. Whisk over low heat until thickened. Grate the cheeses.

To assemble, preheat broiler and grease a large ovenproof casserole. Sprinkle with half of the Parmesan cheese. Spread a thin layer of the cream sauce over cheese. Place half of the scrambled eggs on top. Stir half of the remaining cream sauce into mushrooms; pour mushroom mixture over eggs. Sprinkle with half of the Swiss and Cheddar cheeses. Add rest of eggs. Top with remaining cream sauce. Sprinkle with remaining cheeses. Broil 6" (15 cm) from heat until cheese is bubbly and eggs are heated through. Can be made up to 1 day ahead and refrigerated. Bring to room temperature before broiling, or remove from refrigerator and bake at 350°F (180°C) for 30-45 minutes.

Serves 6-8

Eggs Benedict

Hollandaise Sauce:

½ cup	butter	125 mL
2	egg yolks	2
1 tsp.	lemon juice	5 mL
⅓ cup	boiling water	75 mL
dash	EACH salt, cayenne pepper	dash
12	thin slices ham OR back bacon	12
6	eggs, poached	6
6	English muffins, split, toasted and buttered	6

To make Hollandaise Sauce, divide butter into thirds. Beat egg yolks with lemon juice in the top of a double boiler, then add ⅓ of the butter. Place over simmering, not boiling, water; cook, beating constantly, until butter melts and sauce starts to thicken; add the remaining butter, half at a time, the same way. Beat in boiling water slowly; continue cooking and stirring, still over simmering water, 3 minutes, or until mixture thickens; remove from water. Stir in salt and cayenne pepper; cover sauce and keep warm in double boiler.

Grill bacon or ham and reserve.

To poach eggs, pour water into a large skillet to make a 2" (5 cm) depth; salt lightly; bring just to boil. Break eggs, one at a time into a cup, and slip into water. Simmer, basting often with water in skillet, about 3 minutes, or just until egg is set. Lift out with slotted spoon. Place 2 English muffin halves on each of 6 serving plates. Top each half with a slice of bacon or ham and a poached egg. Spoon sauce over eggs.

Serves 6

Variation: **Blender Hollandaise:** Combine egg yolks, lemon juice, salt and cayenne in a blender or food processor. Do not use the boiling water above. Melt the butter in a pan or in the microwave, until butter is bubbling. Blend egg yolk mixture on high for 30 seconds. Through the feed tube, slowly pour in hot butter and blend until thick. To double – for 1 cup (250 mL) of butter, use 3 egg yolks and the juice of ½ a lemon (1 tbsp. [15 mL]).

Overnight Wine and Cheese Omelet

The perfect make-ahead dish for a busy hostess.

1	small loaf day-old French bread, broken into pieces OR cubed	1
3 tbsp.	butter OR margarine, melted	45 mL
2 cups	shredded Swiss cheese	500 mL
1 cup	shredded Monterey Jack cheese	250 mL
6-8	slices, cooked ham	6-8
8	eggs	8
1½ cups	half and half cereal cream	375 mL
¼ cup	dry white wine	60 mL
3	green onions, chopped	3
2 tsp.	prepared mustard	10 mL
⅛ tsp.	pepper	0.5 mL
dash	cayenne pepper	dash
1 cup	sour cream	250 mL
½-¾ cup	grated Parmesan cheese	125-175 mL

Butter a 9 x 13" (23 x 33 cm) baking dish. Spread bread over the bottom and drizzle with the melted butter. Sprinkle with the shredded cheeses. Arrange ham slices on top of cheese layer. In a large bowl, beat together eggs, cream, wine, green onions, mustard and peppers until foamy. Pour over the casserole. Tightly cover dish with foil. Refrigerate overnight.

Place casserole in a cold oven. Set oven to 325°F (160°C). Bake covered casserole until set, about 1 hour. Uncover; spread with sour cream and sprinkle with Parmesan cheese. Bake, uncovered, until crusty and lightly browned, about 10-15 minutes. Remove from oven and let set for 5-10 minutes before serving.

Serves 6

Christmas Morning Italian Strata

A superb make-ahead dish with an Italian twist.

1½ lbs.	pork sausage meat	750 g
1	loaf French bread	1
2 cups	sliced mushrooms OR 10 oz. (284 mL) canned	500 mL
6	eggs	6
4 cups	milk	1 L
2 tsp.	Italian seasoning	10 mL
1	garlic clove, minced	1
¼ tsp.	pepper	1 mL
2 cups	shredded mozzarella cheese	500 mL
1 cup	shredded Cheddar cheese	250 mL
	chopped parsley for garnish	

In a skillet over medium heat, cook sausage meat, stirring frequently to break up sausage, until thoroughly cooked and no longer pink. Using a slotted spoon, remove sausage to paper towels to drain. Cut French bread into ½" (1.3 cm) cubes. Sauté sliced fresh mushrooms in a little butter, until golden, or drain canned mushrooms. In a greased 9 x 13" (23 x 33 cm) glass baking dish, combine sausage, bread cubes and mushrooms. In a large bowl, whisk together eggs, milk, Italian seasoning, garlic and pepper. Pour egg mixture over the sausage mixture in pan. Cover with plastic wrap and refrigerate overnight.

About 1¾ hours before serving, preheat oven to 350°F (180°C). Bake strata, uncovered, 1 hour. Remove from oven and sprinkle evenly with mozzarella and Cheddar cheeses. Bake 15 minutes longer, or until a knife inserted in the center comes out clean. Remove strata from oven; let stand 10 minutes for easier serving. Garnish with chopped parsley.

Makes 12 main-dish servings

Seafood Brunch Bake

Great for seafood lovers, this lavish dish can be made the night before.

2 cups	sliced mushrooms	500 mL
2 tbsp.	butter OR margarine	30 mL
⅔ cup	sliced green onions	150 mL
4 oz.	can crab meat, drained	113 g
2 x 4 oz.	cans small shrimp, drained and rinsed	2 x 113 g
1 loaf	unsliced day-old bread, cut into 1" (2.5 cm) cubes	1 loaf
2 cups	shredded Monterey Jack cheese, divided	500 mL
⅔ cup	Parmesan cheese, divided	150 mL
8	eggs	8
2 x 13½ oz.	cans evaporated milk	2 x 385 mL
1 tsp.	dry mustard	5 mL
1 tsp.	salt	5 mL
¼ tsp.	nutmeg	1 mL
⅛ tsp.	Tabasco sauce	0.5 mL
⅛ tsp.	pepper	0.5 mL
1 tbsp.	melted butter OR margarine	15 mL
	chopped green onions and chopped parsley for garnish if desired	

Sauté mushrooms in butter, stirring occasionally, until lightly golden. Remove from heat and stir in onions, crab meat and all but ¼ of a can of shrimp (reserve for top). Place half of the bread cubes in a greased 9 x 13" (23 x 33 cm) glass baking dish. Spoon seafood mixture over bread. Sprinkle half of each cheese over seafood. Cover with remaining bread cubes. Whisk together eggs, milk, dry mustard, salt, nutmeg, Tabasco sauce and pepper. Slowly pour egg mixture evenly over casserole. Sprinkle with remaining cheese. Press down lightly. Cover and refrigerate overnight. Bake, uncovered, at 325°F (160°C) for 1 hour. Toss remaining shrimp with melted butter and sprinkle over casserole. Bake for 5 additional minutes. Remove from oven and let stand 5 minutes. Garnish with green onions and parsley if desired. Do not freeze.

Serves 10

Apricot Almond Coffee Cake

The delicate flavors of apricot and almond combine to make this a must for holiday entertaining.

Almond Cinnamon Topping:

1 cup	sliced OR slivered toasted almonds	250 mL
2 tbsp.	sugar	30 mL
1 tsp.	ground cinnamon	5 mL

Apricot Almond Coffee Cake:

½ cup	butter OR margarine, softened	125 mL
1 cup	sugar	250 mL
2	eggs	2
1 tsp.	almond extract	5 mL
1½ cups	flour	375 mL
1½ tsp.	baking powder	7 mL
½ tsp.	salt	2 mL
1 cup	sour cream	250 mL
1 tsp.	baking soda	5 mL
6 oz.	jar apricot preserves	170 mL
	additional toasted almonds (optional)	

Preheat oven to 350°F (180°C). Combine topping ingredients and sprinkle a third of the mixture in the bottom of a well-greased and floured 9" (23 cm) springform pan with a flat bottom. In a small bowl, combine the sour cream and baking soda and set aside. In a large bowl, cream butter and sugar. Add eggs and extract; mix well. Combine flour, baking powder and salt; add to creamed mixture alternately with sour cream mixture. Spoon half over topping in pan. Sprinkle with another third of the topping. Cover with remaining batter and topping. Bake for 60-65 minutes. Cool for 10 minutes. Loosen edges and remove sides of pan. Run a knife around the bottom of the pan. Cool for 10 minutes on a wire rack. Carefully invert onto a serving platter. Spread preserves over top. Garnish with toasted almonds if desired. Serve warm. This freezes well.

Serves 10-12

Pictured on page 85.

Christmas Pull-Aparts

This "gooey" cinnamon maple topping makes these unbeatable for flavor and presentation.

Dough:

3 cups	flour	750 mL
3 tbsp.	sugar	45 mL
1 tbsp.	quick-rise instant yeast (7 g env.)	15 mL
1 tsp.	salt	5 mL
¾ cup	milk	175 mL
¼ cup	water	60 mL
2 tbsp.	butter OR margarine	30 mL
1	egg, beaten lightly	1

Cinnamon-Maple Syrup and Glaze:

¾ cup	maple syrup OR pancake syrup	175 mL
½ cup	coarsely chopped pecans	125 mL
½ cup	whole red and green cherries	125 mL
⅔ cup	sugar	150 mL
2 tsp.	ground cinnamon	10 mL
⅓ cup	butter OR margarine, melted	75 mL

In a large bowl, combine 2¾ cups (675 mL) flour, sugar, yeast and salt. Heat milk, water and butter until hot to touch; stir into dry mixture. Mix in egg and enough of the reserved flour to make a soft dough. Knead on floured surface until smooth, 8-10 minutes. Cover; let rest 10 minutes.

Loaf shaping: In a well-greased 10" (25 cm) tube pan, pour half the syrup and sprinkle the pecans and cherries on bottom. Combine sugar and cinnamon. Divide dough into 32 pieces; roll each into a ball; dip each dough ball in melted butter or margarine and coat with sugar-cinnamon. Layer coated dough balls in pan. Pour the remaining syrup over top. Cover and let rise until doubled in size, about 30-45 minutes. Bake at 375°F (190°C) for 40 minutes, or until lightly browned. Cool in pan on rack for 20 minutes, then remove from pan. Loaf can be wrapped and frozen for up to 1 month.

Makes 1 loaf

Why Not Brunch?
(Holiday Brunch)

Clockwise:
 Orangeberry Muffins, page 92
 Caramel Oven French Toast, page 70
 Christmas Morning Punch, page 98
 Apricot Almond Coffee Cake, page 83
 Crustless Crab Quiche, page 77

Panettone

This Italian Fruit Bread is served at Christmas and for special occasions.

½ cup	milk	125 mL
½ cup	sugar	125 mL
1 tsp.	salt	5 mL
½ cup	butter OR margarine	125 mL
1 tbsp.	active dry yeast (7 g env.)	15 mL
¼ cup	warm water	60 mL
2	eggs	2
2	egg yolks	2
4½ cups	flour	1.125 L
1 tbsp.	grated lemon rind	15 mL
1 cup	golden raisins	250 mL
4 oz.	chopped candied citron	115 g
½ cup	pine nuts	125 mL
2 tbsp.	butter OR margarine	30 mL
	icing sugar	

Combine milk, sugar, salt and ½ cup (125 mL) butter in a small pan. Heat, stirring constantly, until butter melts; cool to lukewarm. Sprinkle yeast into lukewarm water in a large bowl. Stir until yeast dissolves; beat in cooled milk mixture, eggs and egg yolks. Beat in 2 cups (500 mL) of the flour until smooth; stir in lemon rind, raisins, citron and nuts. Stir in 2 more cups (500 mL) of flour to make a soft sticky dough. Turn out onto a floured board; knead until smooth and elastic, adding only enough flour to keep dough from sticking. Place in a greased large bowl; turn to coat all over; cover and let rise in a warm draft-free place, 1½ hours, until double in bulk. Punch dough down and knead in bowl several times; shape into a ball. Press into a greased 8" (20 cm) round cake pan; cover. Let rise again 1½ hours, or until double in bulk. Preheat oven to 350°F (180°C). Cut a shallow cross in top of dough with a sharp knife. Melt remaining 2 tbsp. (30 mL) butter in a small pan. Brush part over dough. Bake for 20 minutes; brush with remaining butter. Bake 25 minutes longer, until loaf sounds hollow when tapped. Remove from pan to a wire rack. Sprinkle with icing sugar. Cool. Slice into wedges; serve warm or cold. Loaf can be wrapped and frozen for up to 1 month.

Makes 1, 8" (20 cm) loaf of bread

Cherry Almond Wreath

This wreath looks beautiful on a Christmas brunch buffet. It has a subtle blending of lemon, cardamom and almond flavors.

Bread:

1 tbsp.	active dry yeast (7 g env.)	15 mL
½ cup	warm milk	125 mL
¼ cup	warm water	60 mL
3-4¼ cups	flour	750 mL-1.06 L
2	eggs	2
¼ cup	butter OR margarine, softened	60 mL
3 tbsp.	sugar	45 mL
1½ tsp.	salt	7 mL
1 tsp.	grated lemon peel	5 mL
½ tsp.	ground cardamom	2 mL

Cherry Almond Filling:

¼ cup	butter OR margarine, softened	60 mL
¼ cup	flour	60 mL
2 tbsp.	sugar	30 mL
1 tsp.	almond extract	5 mL
½ tsp.	grated lemon peel	2 mL
⅔ cup	finely chopped blanched almonds	150 mL
½ cup	chopped red and green candied cherries	125 mL

Lemon Glaze:

⅔ cup	icing sugar	150 mL
2 tsp.	lemon juice	10 mL
1 tsp.	water	5 mL

In a large mixing bowl, dissolve yeast in milk and water. Add 2 cups (500 mL) flour, eggs, butter, sugar, salt, lemon peel and cardamom; beat until smooth. Add enough flour to form a soft dough. Turn onto a floured surface and knead until smooth and elastic, about 6-8 minutes. Place in a greased bowl, turning once to grease top. Cover and let rise in a warm place until doubled, about 1½ hours.

Cherry Almond Wreath

Continued

To make filling, in a small mixing bowl, beat butter, flour, sugar, extract and lemon peel. Stir in almonds and cherries. Refrigerate until needed.

To assemble, punch dough down, roll into a 9 x 30" (23 x 75 cm) rectangle. Crumble filling over dough, distributing evenly. Starting with the long edge, roll up and seal edge. Place, seam side down, on a greased baking sheet. With a sharp knife, cut roll in half lengthwise, carefully turn cut sides up. Loosely twist strips around each other, keeping cut sides up. Shape into a ring and pinch ends together. Cover and let rise 1 hour. Bake at 350°F (180°C) for 35-40 minutes, or until browned. Cool 15 minutes. Combine glaze ingredients and drizzle over warm coffee cake. Cool completely. Coffee cake can be frozen without the glaze for up to 1 month. When ready to serve, thaw, reheat in 350°F (180°C) oven for 10-15 minutes, glaze and serve.

Makes 1 coffee cake

Christmas Stockings

The tradition of hanging up stockings for Christmas started with Saint Nicholas, who was a bishop in Greece. According to legend, Saint Nicholas dropped a purse of gold down the chimney of a poor man who had three beautiful daughters but no money for their dowries, so the girls could not be married. When the bishop dropped the gold, it landed in a stocking the oldest daughter had hung up to dry. Now she had a dowry. The bishop repeated his generous gifts when the other daughters hung up their stockings. Over time, the custom spread and children hung up stockings at Christmas in the hopes that they would be filled with candies and presents.

Stollen

(German Christmas Bread)

Bread:

½ cup	sultana raisins, washed and dried	125 mL
¼ cup	currants, washed and dried	60 mL
1 tbsp.	cognac	15 mL
⅓ cup	lukewarm water	75 mL
2½ tbsp.	sugar	37 mL
1 tbsp.	dry yeast (7 g env.)	15 mL
3½ cups	flour	875 mL
1	lemon, finely grated peel of	1
1	egg	1
½ cup	milk, at room temperature	125 mL
⅓ cup	melted butter, cooled to room temperature	75 mL
½ cup	candied mixed peel	125 mL
½ cup	chopped blanched almonds	125 mL

Marzipan *(commercial Marzipan may be substituted):*

1⅓ cups	ground almonds	325 mL
⅓ cup	icing sugar	75 mL
½ cup	berry sugar	125 mL
2 tbsp.	rose water	30 mL
1	egg yolk	1
¼ cup	melted butter	60 mL
1 tbsp.	icing sugar	15 mL

Place raisins and currants in a small bowl. Stir in cognac; cover and leave at room temperature for at least 4 hours or overnight.

When ready to make bread, pour lukewarm water into a small bowl. Add 1½ tsp. (7 mL) sugar and stir until dissolved. Sprinkle yeast over top. Do not stir. Let stand for 10 minutes, until foamy on top. Meanwhile, measure 2½ cups (625 mL) flour into a large mixing bowl. Add remaining 2 tbsp. (30 mL) sugar. Sprinkle with lemon peel. Stir until well mixed.

Stollen

Continued

In a separate bowl, whisk egg with milk at room temperature. Gradually whisk in melted, cooled butter. When yeast is foamy, stir with a fork. Stir into milk mixture. Make a well in center of flour mixture. Add milk mixture. Stir with a wooden spoon until blended. Stir in marinated raisins and currants, including cognac. Stir in peel and almonds. Gradually stir in ¾ cup (175 mL) of remaining flour until dough forms a ball. Lightly flour a board and place ball of dough on board. Using lightly floured hands, knead dough, working in more flour as needed, until it forms a smooth satiny ball, about 10-15 minutes of kneading. Place dough ball in a large greased bowl; turn to grease top; cover with waxed paper and a damp cloth. Let stand in a warm place until doubled in size, about 1½ hours.

To prepare marzipan, in a medium bowl, stir ground almonds with icing sugar and berry sugar until well blended, then stir in rose water and egg yolk. Marzipan will be fairly firm. Place on a large sheet of waxed paper and roll into a 1 x 15" (2.5 x 38 cm) log. Wrap waxed paper around log. Place in refrigerator until ready to use.

On a lightly floured surface, roll or pat dough into a 8 x 15" (20 x 38 cm) oval. Place cold marzipan log lengthwise in half of oval closest to you. Fold other side of dough over marzipan log. Seal seam well by pinching with fingers. Brush with melted butter if necessary.

Place stollen seam-side down on a lightly greased baking sheet. Brush with melted butter. Cover with greased waxed paper and a damp cloth. Let stand in a warm place until nearly doubled, about 1½ hours.

Preheat oven to 350°F (180°C). Bake stollen in center of oven for about 35 to 40 minutes, or just until golden, then cover with foil and continue to bake for 30 minutes more. Remove from oven and brush with remaining butter. Set aside on a wire rack to cool. Just before serving, dust with icing sugar. Wrap well and store in the refrigerator. Serve at room temperature or warm slightly. This stollen also freezes well.

Makes 1 large loaf

Piña Colada Muffins

Coconut and rum flavors give you a taste of the tropics – just like the drink!

1	egg	1
14 oz.	crushed pineapple, drained	398 mL
½ cup	sour cream	125 mL
½ cup	sugar	125 mL
¼ cup	butter OR margarine, melted	60 mL
¼ cup	rum	60 mL
1½ cups	flour	375 mL
2 tsp.	baking powder	10 mL
½ tsp.	EACH baking soda, salt	2 mL
¾ cup	shredded coconut	175 mL
12	maraschino cherries, finely chopped	12

Preheat oven to 400°F (200°C). In a medium-sized mixing bowl, beat egg lightly; stir in drained pineapple, sour cream, sugar, melted butter and rum. Measure flour, baking powder, baking soda and salt into a large mixing bowl. Stir with a fork until well mixed, then make a well in the center. Pour in pineapple mixture, stirring just until combined. Fold in coconut and cherries. Spoon batter into 12 well-greased medium-sized muffin cups. Bake for 25-30 minutes, or until a pale golden color. Remove from oven; let stand 5 minutes, then turn muffins out onto a cooling rack. These freeze well.

Makes 12 muffins

Orangeberry Muffins

1	whole medium orange, cut into pieces (do not peel)	1
⅓ cup	shortening	75 mL
1	egg	1
½ cup	milk	125 mL
1½ cups	flour	375 mL
¾ cup	sugar	175 ml
2 tsp.	baking powder	10 mL
1 tsp.	baking soda	5 mL
1 cup	frozen OR fresh blueberries	250 mL

Orangeberry Muffins
Continued

Preheat oven to 375°F (190°C). Place orange pieces, shortening, egg and milk in blender or food processor. Blend until orange is finely chopped; set aside. Combine remaining ingredients, except blueberries. Add orange mixture to the dry ingredients and mix only until dry ingredients are moistened. Fold in blueberries. Spoon batter into large, well-greased muffin cups. Bake for 22-25 minutes, or until golden brown. Cool in pan 10 minutes before removing from pan. Place muffins on wire rack and cool completely. These freeze well.

Makes 12 muffins

Variation: Substitute dates, cranberries or Saskatoons for blueberries. Cranberries and Saskatoons need ¼ cup (60 mL) more sugar.

Pictured on page 85.

Cranberry Muffins

2 cups	flour	500 mL
1 cup	sugar	250 mL
1½ tsp.	baking powder	7 mL
½ tsp.	baking soda	2 mL
1 tsp.	salt	5 mL
¼ cup	butter OR margarine	60 mL
¾ cup	orange juice	175 mL
1 tbsp.	grated orange rind	15 mL
1	egg, well beaten	1
½ cup	chopped walnuts OR pecans	125 mL
1 cup	coarsely chopped cranberries	250 mL

Preheat oven to 350°F (180°C). Combine flour, sugar, baking powder, baking soda and salt with a fork. Cut in butter. Combine orange juice and rind with well-beaten egg. Pour into dry ingredients. Mix just to moisten. Fold in nuts and cranberries. Spoon into 12 well-greased medium-sized muffin cups. Bake 25-30 minutes. Cool in pan for 5 minutes; turn out onto a cooling rack. These freeze well.

Makes 12 muffins

Cranberry Fruit Bread

Colorful, moist and delicious, this is perfect for a Christmas brunch.

12 oz.	fresh OR frozen cranberries	340 g
2 cups	chopped pecans	500 mL
1 cup	chopped candied mixed fruit	250 mL
1 cup	chopped dates	250 mL
1 cup	golden raisins	250 mL
1 tbsp.	grated orange peel	15 mL
4 cups	flour, divided	1 L
2 cups	sugar	500 mL
1 tbsp.	baking powder	15 mL
1 tsp.	baking soda	5 mL
¼ tsp.	salt	1 mL
2	eggs	2
1 cup	orange juice	250 mL
¼ cup	shortening, melted	60 mL
¼ cup	warm water	60 mL

Preheat oven to 350°F (180°C). Combine cranberries, pecans, fruit, dates, raisins and orange peel with ¼ cup (60 mL) flour; set aside. In another bowl, combine sugar, baking powder, baking soda, salt and remaining flour; set aside. In a large mixing bowl, beat eggs. Add orange juice, shortening and water. Add flour mixture; stir just until combined. Fold in cranberry mixture. Spoon into 3, 5 x 9" (13 x 23 cm) greased loaf pans. Bake for 60-65 minutes, or until firm to the touch. Remove from oven and set on rack to cool. Loaves can be wrapped and stored for up to 1 week or frozen for up to 3 months.

Makes 3 loaves

Christmas Traditions

American Indians used to believe that on Christmas Eve the deer kneel and look up to the Great Spirit.

Holiday Cheer

Beverages

Wassail Bowl with Baked Apples

The beautiful presentation and wonderful aromas of this punch give a lift to any holiday gathering.

3	apples, cored	3
16 cups	apple cider (1 gallon)	4 L
6	whole cloves	6
6	whole allspice	6
2 tsp.	ground nutmeg	10 mL
6 oz.	frozen lemonade concentrate	178 mL
6 oz.	frozen orange juice concentrate	178 mL
1 cup	packed brown sugar	250 mL
	cinnamon sticks	

Preheat oven to 350°F (180°C). Core apples but do not peel, cut in half crosswise and place, cut side down, in a 9 x 13" (23 x 33 cm) baking dish. Bake for 25 minutes, or until the apple halves are fork-tender. In a large saucepan, over low heat, combine 2 cups (500 mL) apple cider, cloves, allspice and nutmeg. Simmer for 10 minutes. Add remaining apple cider, undiluted lemonade and orange juice concentrates and brown sugar; heat until hot, but not boiling, stirring occasionally. Pour hot cider mixture into a heated large punch bowl. Float apples, skin side up, in punch; sprinkle tops with a little sugar. To serve, ladle into mugs or heat-proof cups and add a cinnamon stick to each.

Makes 18 cups (4.5 L) or 36 half-cup (125 mL) servings

Pictured on page 103.

Variations:

Using "hard" cider will make a punch with an alcohol content; using "soft" or "sweet" cider will make a nonalcoholic punch.

✵ Christmas Traditions ✵

The word "Xmas" got its origin from "X", an abbreviation of Christ coming from the Greek letter x (ch), which begins His name.

Hot Mulled Wine

This full-bodied spicy wine is great after any outdoor activity.

4 cups	sugar	1 L
1 tbsp.	ground cinnamon OR 6 cinnamon sticks	15 mL
1 tsp.	ground cloves OR whole cloves	5 mL
2 cups	boiling water	500 mL
3	oranges, thinly sliced	3
1	lemon, thinly sliced	1
16 cups	dry red wine (1 gallon)	4 L

In an 8-quart (8 L) saucepan, combine sugar, cinnamon, cloves and water. Add orange and lemon slices. Over high heat, heat to boiling; boil 5 minutes, stirring occasionally. Reduce heat to medium; add wine; heat until piping hot, but not boiling, stirring occasionally. Lower heat to simmer to keep warm. Carefully ladle individual servings of hot wine into mugs or heat-safe glasses.

Makes 18 cups (250 mL) or 36 half-cup (125 mL) servings

Hot Cappuccino Punch

A wonderful fireside drink.

3 cups	brewed coffee	750 mL
3 cups	half and half cream	750 mL
½ cup	cream of coconut	125 mL
½ cup	rum	125 mL
½ cup	brandy	125 mL

Combine all ingredients in a large saucepan. Cook over medium heat until mixture begins to boil. Remove from heat. Serve immediately.

Makes 10, 6-oz. (170 mL) servings

Christmas Morning Punch

Try this while opening your gifts on Christmas Morning. It also makes a lovely introduction to a holiday brunch, winter or summer.

9 cups	orange juice	2.25 L
3 cups	peach schnapps	750 mL
26 oz.	dry champagne, chilled	750 mL

Combine the orange juice, peach schnapps and champagne. Pour into a punch bowl and add crushed ice or a frozen ice ring.

Makes 20, 6-oz. (170 mL) servings

Pictured on page 85.

Rich Brandied Eggnog

Creamy and delicious.

12	eggs, separated	12
1 cup	sugar	250 mL
½ cup	brandy	125 mL
1½ cups	rum OR rye	375 mL
2 cups	half and half cream	500 mL
2 cups	milk	500 mL
2 cups	whipping cream	500 mL
1½ tsp. plus	ground nutmeg	6 mL plus

In a large bowl with the mixer at low speed, beat egg yolks with sugar. At high speed, beat until thick and lemon-colored, about 15 minutes, frequently scraping bowl. Carefully beat in brandy and rum, 1 tbsp. (15 mL) at a time to prevent curdling the mixture. Cover and chill. About 20 minutes before serving, in punch bowl stir yolk mixture, milk, half and half and 1¼ tsp. (6 mL) nutmeg. In a large bowl with mixer at high speed, beat egg whites until stiff. Beat whipping cream in another large bowl until stiff peaks form; then fold in egg whites. With wire whisk, gently fold egg whites and cream into the yolk mixture until just blended. To serve, sprinkle some nutmeg over the eggnog; ladle into punch cups.

Makes 20 punch cup servings

Creamy Eggnog

A delicious nonalcoholic eggnog version.

6	eggs, separated	6
2 cups	whole milk	500 mL
1 cup	half and half cereal cream	250 mL
2 cups	vanilla ice cream, softened	500 mL
2 tsp.	vanilla extract	10 mL
1 tsp.	rum extract	5 mL
	nutmeg	

In a large bowl beat egg yolks until light, stir in milk, half and half, ice cream, vanilla and rum extract. In a separate bowl, beat egg whites until stiff. Fold into eggnog and sprinkle with nutmeg.

Makes 10 punch cup servings

Orange Cream

This flavorful drink topped with whipped cream is a dessert and after-dinner beverage all in one.

4 cups	orange juice	1 L
3	cinnamon sticks	3
1 tsp.	vanilla extract	5 mL
1 pint	vanilla ice cream	500 mL
1 cup	whipping cream, whipped	250 mL

In a large saucepan, combine orange juice, cinnamon sticks and vanilla over medium-high heat. Bring mixture to a boil and reduce to low heat. Simmer 10 minutes. Remove cinnamon sticks. Stir in ice cream. Cook over low heat, stirring constantly, until heated through. Do not allow mixture to boil. Top with whipped cream.

Makes 6, 6-oz. (170 mL) servings

Pineapple Julius

½ cup	frozen orange juice concentrate, thawed	125 mL
½ cup	EACH milk and water	125 mL
¼ cup	sugar	60 mL
½ tsp.	vanilla	2 mL
1¾ cups	crushed pineapple	425 mL
1 cup	crushed ice	250 ml

Combine all ingredients in a blender; blend until frothy. Serve at once.
Makes 4 cups (1 L)

Mistletoe Punch

2 x 10 oz.	jars raspberry jelly	2 x 300 mL
2 cups	boiling water	500 mL
12 oz.	frozen orange juice concentrate, thawed	355 mL
1½ qts.	7-Up OR ginger ale, chilled	1.5 L
10 oz.	pkg. frozen strawberries, thawed	283 g

Beat jelly until smooth. Gradually add boiling water and beat until jelly has dissolved. Stir in orange juice concentrate. Chill. To serve, pour chilled raspberry mixture in a punch bowl. Add chilled 7-Up or ginger ale. Garnish with strawberries.
Makes about 24, 4-oz. (125 mL) servings

Golden Glow Punch

4 cups	unsweetened orange juice, chilled	1 L
1 cup	lemon juice, chilled	250 mL
3 cups	unsweetened pineapple juice, chilled	750 mL
2 x 2-qt.	bottles 7-Up OR ginger ale	2 x 2 L
	orange and lemon slices	

Combine all ingredients, except fruit, in a punch bowl in order given. Add ice cubes. Float fruit slices on top. Gin or vodka may be added.
Makes 36, 4-oz. (125 mL) servings

Merry Beginnings

Appetizers

Soups

Savory Cheesecake Pâté

Even people who don't like liver will love this. Make it a day in advance and refrigerate, the flavors develop and ripen overnight.

1 cup	crushed seasoned croûtons	250 mL
3 tbsp.	butter OR margarine, melted	45 mL
1 tbsp.	unflavored gelatin (7 g env.)	15 mL
½ cup	cold water	125 mL
2 x 8 oz.	cream cheese, softened	2 x 250 g
8 oz.	liver sausage	250 g
¼ cup	mayonnaise	60 mL
3 tbsp.	chopped pimiento	45 mL
2 tbsp.	chopped onion	30 mL
1 tbsp.	prepared mustard	15 mL
1 tsp.	lemon juice	5 mL
½ tsp.	garlic salt	2 mL
6-8 drops	hot pepper sauce	6-8 drops

Preheat oven to 350°F (180°C). Combine crumbs and butter, press into the bottom of a 9" (23 cm) springform pan. Bake for 10 minutes. Cool. Soften gelatin in cold water, stir over low heat until dissolved. In a large bowl, beat cream cheese and liver sausage with an electric mixer. Gradually beat in dissolved gelatin. Mix in remaining ingredients. Pour over crust; chill until firm or overnight. To serve, remove pan rim and garnish top. Serves 20.

Pictured opposite.

Simply Delicious Cheese Ball

Make 2-3 days ahead to allow flavors to blend.

16 oz.	cream cheese	500 g
8 oz.	Cheddar cheese (old OR well aged)	250 g
2 tbsp.	chopped green pepper	30 mL
3 tbsp.	chopped onion	45 mL
1 tbsp.	Worcestershire sauce	15 mL
2 tsp.	lemon juice	10 mL
⅛ tsp.	cayenne pepper	0.5 mL
	chopped pecans	

Holiday Cheer & Merry Beginnings
(Appetizer Party)

Clockwise:
Wassail Bowl with Baked Apples, page 96
Spinach Dip, page 105
Broccoli and Cheese Tarts, page 109
Crab-Stuffed Mushrooms, page 108
Oriental Chicken Wings, page 108
Savory Cheesecake Pâté, page 102

Simply Delicious Cheese Ball

Continued

Soften cream cheese and shred the Cheddar. Combine all ingredients, except pecans, using an electric mixer or food processor. Chill until workable. Divide cheese mixture into 3 parts and roll into balls, then roll in pecans. You may also use this as a pâté or spread. Omit the pecans, and place in a pâté dish or serving bowl. This may be made 1 week in advance and kept in the refrigerator.

Variations:

 Each cheese ball could have a different coating: try chopped chives, poppy seed, parsley, etc.

Spinach Dip

This easy, make-ahead creamy dip is always very popular.

10 oz.	pkg. frozen chopped spinach, thawed, squeezed dry	283 g
1 cup	sour cream	250 mL
1 cup	mayonnaise	250 mL
1½ oz.	pkg. ~~vegetable~~ LIPTON ONION soup mix	45 g
4	green onions, chopped	4
8 oz.	can water chestnuts, chopped pepper and salt to taste	227 mL
1 loaf	round pumpernickel bread OR 1 round French loaf	1 loaf

Thaw spinach and squeeze out excess liquid. Combine with remaining ingredients, except bread, and let chill overnight to blend flavors. Cut a slice off the top of the bread and cut in pieces. Remove inside of bread, leaving a 1" (2.5 cm) wall, and cut in pieces. Put the dip in the bread shell and serve on a plate surrounded by bread pieces and crackers. You can make this 1-2 days in advance and refrigerate.

Serves 10-15

Pictured on page 103.

Tuna Mold

Speckled with red pimiento and green celery,
this creamy pâté looks very festive.

10 oz.	can cream of mushroom soup	284 mL
8 oz.	cream cheese, softened	250 g
½ cup	cold water	125 mL
2 tbsp.	unflavored gelatin (2, 7g env.)	30 mL
1 cup	mayonnaise	250 mL
1 cup	finely chopped celery	250 mL
½ cup	finely chopped onion	125 mL
3 tbsp.	finely chopped pimiento	45 mL
2 x 7 oz.	cans tuna	2 x 170 g

Heat soup over low heat; add cheese and stir until the cheese has dissolved. Soften gelatin in cold water; stir over low heat until dissolved, and add to the soup and cheese mixture. Add remaining ingredients and pour into a mold that has been greased with mayonnaise. Refrigerate until set or overnight.

Serves 10-15

Shrimp and Cheese Spread

The traditional version of this easy and popular appetizer uses seafood sauce,
but salsa gives more texture and added flavor – choose your favorite.

½ cup	sour cream	125 mL
8 oz.	cream cheese, softened	250 g
¼ cup	mayonnaise	60 mL
2 x 4½ oz.	cans broken shrimp, rinsed and drained	2 x 128 g
1 cup	salsa OR seafood cocktail sauce	250 mL
2 cups	shredded mozzarella cheese	500 mL
1	green pepper, finely chopped	1
1	tomato, diced	1
3	green onions, finely chopped	3

Shrimp and Cheese Spread

Continued

Mix the first 3 ingredients together. Spread over a 12" (30 cm) plate or serving dish. Scatter shrimp over cheese mixture; add layers of salsa or seafood cocktail sauce and mozzarella cheese and top with green peppers, tomatoes and green onions. Cover and chill until ready to serve. Supply assorted crackers and spoons or pâté knives for spreading. This can be made 1-2 days in advance.

Serves 10-15

Variation:

 2 x 4 oz. (113 g) cans of crab meat, drained, may be substituted for the shrimp or use a mixture of shrimp and crab.

Crab Swiss Spread

This mild-flavored spread will be very popular with all your guests.

8 oz.	cream cheese, softened	250 g
2 x 4 oz.	cans crab meat	2 x 113 g
1 cup	grated, Swiss cheese	250 mL
1 tbsp.	chopped green onion	15 mL
1 tsp.	lemon juice	5 mL
½ cup	mayonnaise	125 mL
¼ tsp.	curry powder	1 mL
	blanched, slivered almonds (optional)	

Preheat oven to 350°F (180°C). Mix all ingredients, except almonds, and place in a lightly buttered casserole. Bake until bubbly, approximately 15 minutes. Remove and sprinkle almonds on top. Bake for 5 more minutes. Serve hot with assorted crackers.

Serves 10-15

Note:

 This spread can be made earlier in the day and refrigerated if desired. Bake just before serving.

Crab-Stuffed Mushrooms

1 lb.	mushrooms	500 g
2 x 4 oz.	cans crab meat	2 x 113 g
1	egg, well beaten	1
¼ cup	fine bread crumbs	60 mL
¼ cup	tomato juice	60 mL
1 tsp.	lemon juice	5 mL
dash	Tabasco	dash
1 tsp.	finely chopped onion	5 mL
2 tsp.	finely chopped celery	10 mL
½ tsp.	salt	2 mL
½ cup	bread crumbs	125 mL
¼ cup	melted butter OR margarine	60 mL

Clean mushrooms; remove and chop stems. Mix together chopped stems, crab, egg, ¼ cup (60 mL) crumbs, tomato juice, lemon juice, Tabasco, onion, celery and salt. Fill mushroom caps with the crab mixture. Toss the remaining bread crumbs with the melted butter. Sprinkle over the mushroom caps. Place caps on a baking sheet. Cover with foil and refrigerate until ready to cook. Remove foil. Broil 6" (15 cm) from heat for 5-8 minutes, or until crumbs are lightly browned, or bake at 350°F (180°C) for 15-20 minutes. Mushrooms may be stuffed early in the day and refrigerated until ready to heat and serve.

Serves 6-8

Pictured on page 103.

Oriental Chicken Wings

1	garlic clove, minced	1
1 tbsp.	oil	15 mL
1 tsp.	ginger	5 mL
2 tbsp.	ketchup	30 mL
½ cup	hamburger relish	125 mL
¼ cup	honey	60 mL
3 tbsp.	orange juice	45 mL
2 tbsp.	lemon juice	30 mL
1 tbsp.	soy sauce	15 mL
2 lbs.	chicken wings (about 12 wings)	1 kg

Oriental Chicken Wings
Continued

Preheat oven to 375°F (190°C). Sauté garlic in oil. Add all other ingredients, except wings; simmer on low for 15 minutes. Remove wing
tips; discard or save for stock, cut wings into 2 parts; put in a large
glass dish. Pour sauce over the wings; marinate in refrigerator at least
2 hours or overnight, stirring occasionally. Place chicken on foil-lined
baking sheet. Brush with marinade. Bake for 40 minutes, basting occasionally. Remove from oven; place on a platter; serve immediately.

Serves 10-12

Pictured on page 103.

Broccoli and Cheese Tarts

	pastry for 2-crust pie	
2 tbsp.	butter OR margarine, melted	30 mL
¾ cup	finely chopped fresh OR frozen broccoli, partially cooked	175 mL
¾ cup	shredded Swiss cheese	175 mL
1 cup	half and half cereal cream	250 mL
3	eggs	3
1 tsp.	salt	5 mL
⅛ tsp.	pepper	0.5 mL

Grease and flour 36, 1¾" (4.5 cm) muffin pans. On a lightly floured surface, with a floured rolling pin, roll dough about ⅛" (3 mm) thick. Using
3" (7 cm) round cookie cutter, cut dough into 36 circles, re-rolling pastry
scraps. Line muffin pans with pastry circles; brush lightly with melted
butter; refrigerate 30 minutes. Preheat oven to 400°F (200°C). Drain broccoli on paper towels. Into each muffin pan, spoon about 1 tsp. (5 mL)
broccoli and top with some shredded cheese. In a small bowl with a wire
whisk, mix well the cream, eggs, salt and pepper. Spoon about 1 tbsp.
(15 mL) egg mixture into each pan. Bake 25 minutes, or until knife
inserted in center of a tart comes out clean. Remove from pan and serve.

Makes 36 appetizers

Pictured on page 103.

Variation:

Spinach Tarts: Use frozen chopped spinach, instead of broccoli.

Christmas Sauerkraut Soup

This thick, rich, flavorful soup is made traditionally by Mom Mandryk for Christmas Eve.

1	large potato, peeled, cooked, mashed	1
2 tbsp.	onion soup mix	30 mL
2½ cups	chicken stock	625 mL
96 oz.	jar sauerkraut, drained and rinsed	3 L
1	medium onion, chopped	1
½ cup	butter	125 mL
2 tbsp.	flour	30 mL
½ cup	whipping cream	125 mL

Peel, cook and mash potato. In a large saucepan, combine onion soup mix, chicken broth and washed sauerkraut; heat over medium heat. In a skillet over low heat, cook onion in butter until tender. Add flour, stirring constantly, and continue cooking for 1-2 minutes. Add the whipping cream, stirring constantly. Add the cream mixture to the sauerkraut mixture; then add the mashed potato. Simmer over low heat until sauerkraut is soft. Stir frequently to prevent burning.

Serves 10-12

French Canadian Pea Soup

1 cup	dry split peas	250 mL
3 cups	cold water	750 mL
2 lbs.	smoked ham shank OR a ham bone	1 kg
1	onion, thinly sliced	1
3 qts.	boiling water	3 L
2	carrots, shredded	2
2 cups	chopped celery	500 mL
1 tsp.	salt	5 mL
⅛ tsp.	pepper	0.5 mL

Soak the peas in cold water overnight; drain. Combine the peas, ham, onion and boiling water. Cover, bring to a boil; simmer 2-3 hours, stirring often to prevent sticking. During the last hour of cooking add the carrots, celery and seasonings. Serve immediately.

Serves 8-10

French Onion Soup

Caramelized onions and savory beefy flavors stimulate the taste buds.

4-5	large yellow onions (about 1½ lbs. [750 g])	4-5
¼ cup	butter OR margarine	60 mL
2 tbsp.	sugar	30 mL
2 tbsp.	flour	30 mL
⅛ tsp.	pepper	0.5 mL
1 tsp.	dried thyme	5 mL
2	garlic cloves, crushed	2
5 cups	beef stock*	1.25 mL
½ cup	dry white wine	125 mL
¼ cup	rye whiskey	60 mL
2 tbsp.	parsley flakes	30 mL
6-8 slices	French bread (croûtons may be used)	6-8 slices
1½ cups	grated Swiss, mozzarella OR Gruyère cheese	375 mL

Peel onions and slice thinly (about 5 cups [1.25 L]). Put butter in a large skillet and heat over moderately high heat until butter melts. Add onions and sauté, stirring frequently with wooden spoon, until onions are a light golden brown, about 10 minutes. Combine in a separate bowl the sugar, flour, pepper, thyme and garlic. Sprinkle over onions; continue frying and stirring constantly until all traces of flour disappear, 2-3 minutes. Remove from heat. In a 4-quart (4 L) saucepan combine stock, wine, rye and parsley.

Gradually add the onions to the broth, stirring constantly. Place on medium-high heat and bring to a boil, stirring constantly. Reduce heat to low simmer for 45-60 minutes.

To serve, pour soup into individual heatproof bowls. Toast French bread in toaster until light golden brown. Arrange toast slices on top of soup. Sprinkle toast liberally with cheese. Bake at 425°F (220°C) until cheese melts and turns golden. Serve immediately.

Serves 4-6

* If you don't have beef stock on hand, substitute beef broth or consommé, 4 x 10-oz. (284 mL) cans.

Sherried Mushroom Soup

A wonderful smooth, rich flavor, try it for Christmas Eve.

¼ cup	butter OR margarine	60 mL
1 cup	chopped onions	250 mL
5 cups	sliced mushrooms	1.25 L
5 cups	beef stock	1.25 L
½ cup	medium dry sherry	125 mL
¼ cup	chopped fresh parsley	60 mL
	seasoned croûtons	
	grated Parmesan cheese	

Melt butter in a large saucepan; sauté onions until tender. Add mushrooms and cook, covered, until moisture is released. Stir in stock and sherry. Bring to a boil; simmer gently for 10 minutes. Stir in parsley and serve with seasoned croûtons and Parmesan cheese, if desired. Serves 8-10

Hearty Clam Chowder

Creamy chowder loaded with clams, this is a meal in itself.

2 x 10 oz.	cans clams	2 x 283 g
3 cups	diced potatoes	750 mL
½ tsp.	sugar	2 mL
½ tsp.	vinegar	2 mL
1½ tsp.	salt	7 mL
¼ cup	butter	60 mL
1 cup	EACH chopped celery and onions	250 mL
¼ cup	flour	60 mL
2 cups	half and half cereal cream	500 mL
2 cups	milk	500 mL
5 slices	bacon, cooked and crumbled (optional)	5 slices

Drain juice from clams and pour over potatoes. Add water to cover. Add sugar, vinegar and salt. Cook until potatoes are tender (do not drain). Melt butter, sauté celery and onions, then add flour. Add cream and milk, stirring constantly. Add potatoes and their liquid; mix thoroughly. Add clams. Garnish with bacon if using. Serve steaming hot with your favorite bread. You can make this 1 day in advance and refrigerate. Reheat and garnish with bacon and serve. Serves 6-8

Yuletide Feasts

Salads
Vegetable Dishes
Main Dishes

Christmas Cranberry Apple Salad

The lovely color of this jellied salad adds a festive look to any holiday table.

3 cups	canned whole cranberry sauce with juice	750 mL
1 tbsp.	gelatin (7 g env.)	15 mL
2 cups	boiling water	500 mL
2 x 3 oz.	pkgs. raspberry gelatin	2 x 85 g
1	lemon, juice of	1
¾ cup	mayonnaise	175 mL
2 cups	finely chopped pared apple	500 mL
½ cup	chopped walnuts (optional)	125 mL

Heat cranberries in a saucepan just to the point where the liquid can be poured off. Drain liquid into a large bowl. Dissolve gelatin in a small dish according to package instructions and stir into the cranberry liquid. Add 2 cups (500 mL) boiling water and the raspberry gelatin. Stir until gelatin dissolves. Stir in lemon juice. Place mixture in the refrigerator to chill until syrupy. Remove from refrigerator and stir in mayonnaise. Beat with electric mixer until smooth. Stir in whole cranberries, chopped apple and walnuts, if using. Pour into a 2-quart (2 L) mold. Chill overnight. Unmold to serve; garnish as desired.

Serves 10-12

Pictured on page 137.

Cranberry Sparkle Salad

The tart zest of cranberries adds flavor and color to this family favorite salad.

½ lb.	fresh cranberries	250 g
1	orange	1
1	lemon	1
1 cup	sugar	250 mL
10 oz.	can crushed pineapple	284 mL
2 cups	diced apples	500 mL
2 x 3 oz.	pkgs. lemon gelatin powder	2 x 85 g
2 cups	boiling water	500 mL
	mayonnaise	

Cranberry Sparkle Salad
Continued

Grind cranberries and combine with grated rind of half the orange. Squeeze juice from the orange and lemon and mix with cranberries. Add sugar and let stand for 2 hours. Add pineapple and apple and set aside. In large bowl dissolve gelatin in boiling water. Chill until it becomes syrupy, then fold in fruit mixture. Pour into a large oiled (vegetable oil) salad mold. Chill until firm or overnight. Unmold on a large plate. Serve with mayonnaise.

Serves 10-12

Golden Glow Salad

Full of fruit and vegetables, colorful and delicious,
this is one of our family favorites.

3 oz.	pkg. lemon gelatin powder	85 g
1 cup	boiling water	250 mL
½ cup	pineapple juice	125 mL
½ cup	mayonnaise	125 mL
1 tbsp.	vinegar	15 mL
1 tsp.	salt	5 mL
½ cup	drained crushed pineapple	125 mL
½ cup	shredded carrots	125 mL
½ cup	finely chopped celery	125 mL
1 tbsp.	finely chopped onion	15 mL
1	apple, cored and chopped (do not peel)	1

In bowl combine gelatin powder and hot water. Stir well to dissolve. Add pineapple juice, mayonnaise, vinegar and salt. Blend together and set in refrigerator until almost set. With electric mixer, beat until fluffy. Stir in pineapple, carrots, celery, onion and apple. Mix well to combine. Pour into a jelly mold and chill until set or overnight. Unmold to serve.

Serves 8-10

Fresh Fruit Salad

1	cantaloupe melon, halved and seeded	1
½	honeydew melon, seeded	½
¼ cup	sugar	60 mL
¼ cup	fresh lime juice	60 mL
2 tbsp.	fresh lemon juice	30 mL
1 tbsp.	orange-flavored liqueur (optional)	15 mL
1½ tsp.	grated lime peel	7 mL
1 cup	sliced fresh strawberries	250 mL
1 cup	green OR red seedless grapes	250 mL

Using a melon baller, scoop flesh from cantaloupe and honeydew into balls and set aside. In a large bowl, combine the sugar, lime juice, lemon juice, orange liqueur and lime peel. Stir well to dissolve sugar. Add the cantaloupe and honeydew balls, strawberries and grapes. Toss gently to combine. Cover the bowl with plastic wrap and refrigerate for at least 1 hour to blend flavors, stirring once or twice. Spoon the fruit mixture into serving bowls or hollowed out melon halves, dividing evenly. Serve immediately.

Serves 6

Variations:

 Tropical Fruit Salad: substitute kiwi slices, pineapple chunks, papaya slices and/or mango cubes for some of the melon balls. Add a little grated fresh ginger or ground ginger. A dash of coconut extract would also make an intriguing addition. Try serving this version in a hollowed-out pineapple half.

 To make a melon basket, use a non-toxic marker to draw a zigzag or scallop pattern on melon, include a handle at the halfway point if you wish. Cut deeply into fruit along pattern, separate halves or portions beside the handle section; remove seeds, hollow out melon and fill with fruit.

Tossed Greens with Raspberry Vinaigrette

This tangy raspberry dressing adds zest to a green salad.

Raspberry Vinaigrette:

½ cup	walnuts (optional)	125 mL
⅓ cup	vegetable oil	75 mL
2½ tbsp.	raspberry vinegar	37 mL
1 tbsp.	chopped onion	15 mL
½ tsp.	salt	2 mL
½ tsp.	sugar	2 mL
2 cups	EACH torn, stemmed Romaine lettuce, spinach, leaf lettuce leaves	500 mL
1 cup	halved red seedless grapes	250 mL

If using walnuts, preheat oven to 350°F (180°C). Toast walnuts, spread in a single layer on baking sheet. Bake 6-8 minutes, or until lightly golden brown, stirring frequently. Remove walnuts from sheet and cool. Coarsely chop and set aside. Place oil, vinegar, onion, salt and sugar in a small bowl or small jar with lid. Whisk together or cover jar and shake until mixed. Cover; refrigerate up to 1 week. Combine greens, grapes and cooled walnuts in a large bowl. Just before serving, add dressing; toss well to coat.

Serves 6-8

Advent Wreaths and Calendars

In Germany and Scandinavian countries, Advent wreaths of fir branches are placed on dining room tables or hung up on Advent Sunday, four weeks before Christmas. Four red or yellow candles are fastened to the wreath and one candle is lit on the first Sunday of Advent, two on the second and so on, by Christmas Day all the candles are lit. In many countries, children use Advent calendars to count off the days before Christmas. Twenty-four dated little paper flaps are opened to see the pictures underneath. The Christmas Eve flap usually shows a shining Christmas tree. Other Advent calendars use a fir wreath with 24 little boxes hung on it. Each numbered box holds a tiny present. One box is opened each day.

Cashew and Orange Salad

This cashew lovers' delight has lots of crunch and a zippy dressing.

½ cup	unsalted cashews	125 mL
3 tbsp.	brown sugar	45 mL
2 tbsp.	water	30 mL
1 head	butter lettuce	1 head
½ head	romaine lettuce	½ head
1 cup	chopped celery	250 mL
2	green onions, chopped	2
1⅓ cups	mandarin orange segments OR peeled orange slices cut into wedges	325 mL

Red Wine Vinegar Dressing:

½ tsp.	salt	2 mL
2 tbsp.	sugar	30 mL
¼ cup	vegetable oil	60 mL
1 tbsp.	chopped parsley	15 mL
2 tbsp.	red wine vinegar	30 mL
dash	Tabasco sauce	dash

In a small pan over medium heat, cook cashews, brown sugar and water, stirring constantly until cashews are coated and sugar dissolved. Do not burn. Cool on waxed paper and store in an airtight container. Combine lettuces, celery and onions.

To prepare the salad dressing, combine all the ingredients, mixing well, or put in a container and shake well. Chill until serving time, then shake thoroughly; pour over salad and add the sugared nuts and oranges.

Serves 4-6

Fire and Ice Tomatoes

This "hot" salad will wake up your taste buds.

6	large ripe firm tomatoes, skinned and quartered	6
1	large green pepper, seeds removed and sliced into strips	1
1	medium onion, sliced into rings	1
1	cucumber, peeled and sliced	1

Peppery Mustard Dressing:

½ cup	vinegar	125 mL
1½ tsp.	celery salt	7 mL
1½ tsp.	mustard seed	7 mL
½ tsp.	salt	2 mL
1½ tsp.	sugar	7 mL
¼ tsp.	crushed red pepper flakes, OR more to taste	1 mL
⅛ tsp.	black pepper	0.5 mL
¼ cup	cold water	60 mL

Combine tomatoes, pepper and onion rings in a large bowl. Stir to combine and set aside until the dressing is prepared.

Combine all dressing ingredients in a large saucepan. Mix well and place over heat. Bring to a boil, boil very rapidly for 1 minute only. While mixture is hot, pour over the tomatoes, peppers and onion rings. Cool.

Just before serving, add the peeled, sliced cucumber. Will keep well refrigerated, without the cucumber, for several days.

Serves 6-8

Variation:

 For a red-green-white mixture, use an English cucumber, unpeeled. For a red-white look (fire & ice) use a sweet red bell pepper instead of the green.

Oriental Shrimp Salad

Crisp fresh textures and flavors, use this salad for lunch or on a buffet table.

Horseradish Garlic Mayonnaise:

¾ cup	mayonnaise	175 mL
¼ cup	lemon juice	60 mL
1 tbsp.	prepared horseradish	15 mL
1	garlic clove, minced	1
1 lb.	small shrimp, peeled, deveined and cooked	500 mL
4 oz.	fresh pea pods OR 10 oz. (283 g) pkg. frozen	125 g
8 oz.	can sliced water chestnuts, drained	227 mL
1 cup	sliced fresh mushrooms	250 mL
1 cup	diagonally sliced celery	250 mL
1 cup	fresh bean sprouts	250 mL
¼ cup	sliced green onions	60 mL

In a large bowl, combine mayonnaise, lemon juice, horseradish and garlic. Add remaining ingredients and mix well. Cover and chill to blend flavors.

Serves 6

Shrimp and Corn Salad

A colorful tangy salad.

12 oz.	can whole kernel corn, drained	341 mL
4 oz.	can tiny shrimp drained and rinsed	113 g
1	small tomato, peeled, seeded and chopped	1
2 tbsp.	finely chopped onion	30 mL
2 tbsp.	snipped parsley	30 mL
¼ cup	sour cream	60 mL
2 tbsp.	chili sauce	30 mL

Shrimp and Corn Salad

Continued

In a medium bowl, combine the corn, shrimp, tomato, onion and parsley. Toss to mix well. Set aside.

For the dressing, in a small bowl, stir together the sour cream and chili sauce. Add to the corn mixture. Toss to coat.

Serves 4-6

Crunchy Broccoli

Sour cream and Parmesan cheese give this a rich creamy flavor.

5 cups	chopped broccoli	1.25 L
¼ cup	chopped onion	60 mL
¼ cup	butter OR margarine	60 mL
1 tbsp.	flour	15 mL
½ tsp.	salt	2 mL
¼ tsp.	pepper	1 mL
1 cup	sour cream	250 mL
¾ cup	bread crumbs	175 mL
¼ cup	Parmesan cheese	60 mL

Preheat oven to 350°F (180°C). Cook broccoli for 4 minutes, drain and place in a 2-quart (2 L) greased casserole. Sauté onions in 2 tbsp. (30 mL) of butter until tender. Blend in flour, salt and pepper. Stir in sour cream; cook until thick; pour cream mixture over broccoli. The mixture can be refrigerated overnight at this point and finished before cooking. Melt remaining butter, remove from heat and stir in bread crumbs. Sprinkle over broccoli and top with cheese. Bake for 25-30 minutes.

Serves 6-8

The Great Green Vegetable Bake

A perfect make-ahead dish.

1 cup	broccoli florets	250 mL
1 cup	chopped green beans	250 mL
1 cup	peas	250 mL
½ cup	chopped onions	125 mL
2 tbsp.	butter OR margarine	30 mL
1-1½ tbsp.	cornstarch	15-22 mL
1 tsp.	salt	5 mL
¼ tsp.	pepper	1 mL
½ cup	sour cream	125 mL
1 cup	grated Cheddar cheese	250 mL
2 tbsp.	butter OR margarine, melted	30 mL
1 cup	crushed Ritz crackers	250 mL

Preheat oven to 350°F (180°C). Steam or boil the broccoli, beans and peas until tender, drain and set aside. Cook onions in 2 tbsp. (30 mL) butter until tender. Add cornstarch, salt, pepper and sour cream; mix well. Stir in green vegetables. Put in a greased 2-quart (2 L) casserole. Mixture can be refrigerated overnight at this point and finished before cooking. Top with grated cheese. Combine remaining 2 tbsp. (30 mL) of butter and cracker crumbs; sprinkle over cheese. Bake for 30 minutes.

Serves 6-8

Green Vegetable Medley

1 lb.	small white onions, peeled	500 g
3 cups	frozen small sweet peas	750 mL
1 lb.	frozen snow peas	500 g
3 tbsp.	butter	45 mL
3-5	garlic cloves, minced	3-5
1 lb.	fresh mushrooms, cleaned, sliced	500 g

Green Vegetable Medley

Continued

In a saucepan over high heat, boil water; add onions; reduce heat to low; cover and cook 10 minutes, or until tender. Drain; cover; set aside. Cook peas in boiling water until tender crisp. Remove from heat; drain and place in colander. Cook frozen snow peas in boiling water until tender crisp. Remove from heat, drain and transfer to colander. In skillet over medium-low heat, melt butter and sauté garlic and mushrooms about 5 minutes, or until tender. Add the peas, snow peas and onions to the mushroom mixture and heat thoroughly, approximately 3 minutes. Transfer to serving dish and serve immediately.

Serves 10-12

Cauliflower and Mushrooms in Cheese Sauce

1-1½ heads	cauliflower	1-1½ heads
1½ cups	sliced mushrooms	375 mL
4 tbsp.	butter	60 mL
3 tbsp.	flour	45 mL
1½ cups	milk	375 mL
½ tsp.	salt	2 mL
⅛ tsp.	pepper	0.5 mL
¼ tsp.	dry mustard	1 mL
1½-2 cups	shredded sharp Cheddar cheese	375-500 mL
	Parmesan cheese	

Preheat oven to 375°F (190°C). Cook cauliflower; drain; rinse in cold water; set aside. In a skillet, sauté mushrooms in 1 tbsp. (15 mL) of butter for 2-3 minutes, or until soft. In a large saucepan, melt remaining butter over medium heat. Stir in flour and cook for 1 minute. Whisk in milk; continue to cook until mixture boils, stirring constantly. Stir in salt, pepper, mustard and cheese. Cook until cheese melts and sauce is smooth. Remove from heat; stir in mushrooms and cauliflower. Mix well. Turn into a 2-quart (2 L) greased casserole. Mixture can be refrigerated overnight at this point and finished before cooking. Sprinkle top with Parmesan cheese. Bake for 30-45 minutes.

Serves 8-10

Cauliflower with Shrimp Sauce

Serve this to impress dinner guests – very elegant and tasty.

1-1½ heads	cauliflower	1-1½ heads

Parmesan Shrimp Sauce:

2 tbsp.	butter OR margarine	30 mL
2 tbsp.	flour	30 mL
½ cup	chicken stock	125 mL
½ cup	whipping cream	125 mL
¼ tsp.	salt	1 mL
¼ tsp.	pepper	1 mL
¼ cup	Parmesan cheese	60 mL
½ lb.	baby shrimp, cooked	250 g
½ cup	sour cream	125 mL
¼ cup	toasted slivered almonds	60 mL
½ cup	bread crumbs	125 mL
¾ cup	grated Cheddar cheese	175 mL

Separate cauliflower into florets. Blanch in boiling water for 4 minutes. Drain and run under cold water until cool. Arrange cauliflower in a greased 2-quart (2 L) casserole and set aside while preparing sauce. Preheat oven to 350°F (180°C).

In a saucepan, melt the butter, add the flour and stir well. Add the chicken stock, cream and seasonings. Simmer, while stirring, until thickened. Add Parmesan cheese and simmer 2 more minutes. Remove from heat and add shrimp and sour cream. Pour over cauliflower. Mixture can be refrigerated overnight at this point and finished before cooking. Sprinkle almonds on top, then bread crumbs and Cheddar cheese. Bake for 30-45 minutes.

Serves 8-10

Cauliflower Tomato Medley

A colorful addition to any Christmas buffet.

1 head	medium cauliflower, medium size	1 head
6	bacon slices, cut in ½" (1.3 cm) pieces	6
3 tbsp.	bacon drippings	45 mL
1½ cups	soft breadcrumbs	375 mL
3	medium tomatoes, sliced	3
2 tbsp.	chopped green onion	30 mL
¼ tsp.	salt	1 mL
⅛ tsp.	pepper	0.5 mL
¼ tsp.	dill seed	1 mL
¾ cup	grated Cheddar cheese	175 mL

Preheat oven to 400°F (200°C). Separate cauliflower into florets and boil until just tender; drain. Meanwhile cook bacon until crisp. Toss crumbs with bacon and measured drippings. Arrange tomatoes in a greased shallow baking dish, about 6-cup (1.5 L) size. Sprinkle with onion, salt, pepper and dill. Add cauliflower; top with crumb mixture. Cover and bake 10 minutes. Uncover and continue baking until tender, about 5 minutes. Sprinkle cheese over top; bake until cheese melts.

Serves 6

 Mistletoe

In Norse mythology it is said that the god Frigga made mistletoe a symbol of love and promised a kiss to all who passed beneath it.

Ancient Celtic priests called Druids had ceremonies where people kissed beneath mistletoe to symbolize forgiveness and the end of old grievances. For the same reason, sprigs of mistletoe were hung over the entrance to the house to bring happiness to everyone who passed under them.

In the 17th Century kissing under the mistletoe came into fashion. The man would pluck a berry from the mistletoe for each kiss and when the berries were gone there was no more kissing.

Spinach Puff

Even people who don't like spinach cannot resist this.

2 x 10 oz.	pkgs. frozen chopped spinach	2 x 283 g
4 oz.	cream cheese, cubed	125 g
3	eggs, well beaten	3
¾ cup	milk	175 mL
¼ tsp.	nutmeg	1 mL
	salt and pepper to taste	
1½ cups	crushed wheat crackers	375 mL
¼ cup	shredded Cheddar cheese	60 mL

Preheat oven to 350°F (180°C). Cook the spinach according to package directions. Drain thoroughly; while spinach is still hot, add cream cheese. Stir over low heat until cheese melts to form a cream sauce. Beat in all other ingredients except cracker crumbs and Cheddar cheese. Grease a 9" (23 cm) square baking pan. Place half of the spinach mixture in the pan. Top with half of the crumbs. Layer the remaining spinach mixture, then Cheddar cheese and finally the remaining crumbs. Bake for 30 minutes, or until puffed and golden.

Serves 8-10

Corn-Mushroom Bake

Truly a crowd pleaser.

¼ cup	flour	60 mL
14 oz.	can cream-style corn	398 mL
3 oz.	cream cheese, cubed	85 g
2 tbsp.	chopped onion	30 mL
12 oz.	can whole kernel corn	341 mL
2 cups	sliced fresh mushrooms OR 10 oz. (284 mL) canned, drained	500 mL
½ cup	shredded Swiss cheese	125 mL
1½ cups	soft bread crumbs	375 mL
3 tbsp.	melted butter	45 mL

Corn-Mushroom Bake

Continued

Preheat oven to 400°F (200°C). In a large saucepan, stir flour into cream-style corn and onion. Add cream cheese. Heat and stir over low heat until cheese melts. Sauté fresh mushrooms until golden. Add drained kernel corn and mushrooms to creamed corn mixture. Stir the Swiss cheese into hot mixture. Pour into a buttered 1½-quart (1.5 L) casserole. Combine the bread crumbs and melted butter, mix well and sprinkle over casserole. Bake for 30 minutes.

Serves 10-12

Golden Carrot Ring

Filled with a green vegetable, these carrots add vibrant color to your dinner table or buffet.

2 tbsp.	butter OR margarine	30 mL
1 cup	sliced fresh mushrooms	250 mL
3	eggs	3
1 cup	evaporated milk	250 mL
½ tsp.	salt	2 mL
½ tsp.	freshly ground pepper	2 mL
2 cups	packed grated raw carrot	500 mL
¼ cup	sliced, toasted almonds (optional)	60 mL
½ cup	chopped green onion	125 mL
	peas OR green beans	

Melt butter in a skillet and sauté mushrooms until most of the liquid released is evaporated. Butter a 4-cup (1 L) ring mold. Preheat oven to 325°F (160°C). Beat eggs lightly. Add milk, salt and pepper. Fold in the mushrooms, carrots, almonds, and onions. Pour the mixture into the mold. Place the mold in a pan of hot water and bake until the ring is firm, 50-60 minutes. Remove from oven and invert onto a serving dish. Fill the center of the ring with cooked frozen peas or green beans.

Serves 6-8

Pictured on page 137.

Holiday Sweet Potatoes

4	large sweet potatoes, boiled, drained and mashed	4
¼ tsp.	salt	1 mL
¼ cup	butter OR margarine, softened	60 mL
2	eggs, lightly beaten	2
1 tsp.	vanilla	5 mL
1 tsp.	cinnamon	5 mL
dash	ginger OR to taste	dash
⅓ cup	sugar	75 mL
¼ cup	butter OR margarine, melted	60 mL
3 tbsp.	flour	45 mL
¾ cup	brown sugar	175 mL
¼ cup	chopped pecans (optional)	60 mL

Preheat oven to 350°F (180°C). Mix together mashed sweet potatoes, salt, butter, eggs, vanilla, cinnamon, ginger and sugar. Pour into greased 1½-quart (1.5 L) casserole. Mix together butter, flour, brown sugar and pecans; pour over potato mixture. Bake for 30 minutes.

Makes 6-8 servings

Holiday Turnips

Turnips are "dressed up" with apple for a Christmas presentation.

1	large turnip (rutabaga)	1
2	apples, peeled and quartered	2
1 tbsp.	butter OR margarine	15 mL
2	eggs, well beaten	2
3 tbsp.	flour	45 mL
1 tbsp.	brown sugar	15 mL
1 tsp.	baking powder	5 mL
½ tsp.	salt	2 mL
⅛ tsp.	EACH pepper, nutmeg	0.5 mL
1 cup	crushed seasoned croûtons	250 mL
3 tbsp.	melted butter	45 mL

Holiday Turnips

Continued

Peel turnip, cut and cube. Peel apples and quarter. Boil together until tender, drain, mash, add butter and well-beaten eggs and beat well. Preheat oven to 350°F (180°C). In a separate bowl, combine flour, sugar, baking powder, salt, pepper and nutmeg. Stir with a fork to combine mixture. Stir flour mixture into the turnip mixture. Combine well and pour into a buttered 2-quart (2 L) casserole. Combine crushed seasoned croûtons with melted butter. Mix well and sprinkle on top. Bake for 30-40 minutes.

Serves 8-10

Potatoes Romanoff

*A great make ahead for a buffet or a delicious way to
use leftover mashed potatoes.*

6	medium potatoes	6
1 cup	sour cream	250 mL
4	green onions, sliced (optional)	4
1¼ cups	shredded sharp Cheddar cheese	300 mL
1 tsp.	salt	5 mL
⅛ tsp.	pepper	0.5 mL
¼ tsp.	paprika	1 mL
¼ cup	shredded sharp Cheddar cheese	60 mL

Peel potatoes, cook in boiling water, drain and mash. Preheat oven to 350°F (180°C). Combine potatoes with all the other ingredients except the ¼ cup (60 mL) cheese. Turn potatoes into a buttered 1½-quart (1.5 L) casserole. Sprinkle with the additional ¼ cup (60 mL) cheese and paprika. Bake for 30-40 minutes. These potatoes can be refrigerated overnight or frozen for 2-3 weeks and baked later.

Serves 6-8

Pictured on page 137.

Whipped Potato Casserole

These can be made weeks ahead of time to save the hostess valuable last-minute preparation time.

10-12	medium potatoes	10-12
¼ cup	butter OR margarine	60 mL
8 oz.	cream cheese, cubed	250 g
1 cup	sour cream	250 mL
	salt and pepper to taste	
2 tbsp.	melted butter	30 mL
¼ cup	dry bread crumbs	60 mL

Cook potatoes in boiling salted water until tender; drain and return to heat briefly to dry. Preheat oven to 350°F (180°C). Mash the potatoes with ¼ cup (60 mL) of butter. Add the cream cheese, sour cream, salt and pepper and beat until creamy. Spoon into a greased 2-quart (2 L) casserole. Combine the melted butter and bread crumbs and sprinkle evenly over the top. Cover tightly and refrigerate until needed. This dish can be made a day or two ahead and refrigerated until needed or it can be frozen for 2-3 weeks. Remove casserole from the refrigerator 30 minutes before reheating (or 3-4 hours if frozen). Bake, uncovered, for 30-45 minutes, or until heated through.

Serves 10

Variation:

 Try grated Cheddar cheese instead of crumbs and melted butter.

 Netherlands Christmas Traditions

The Christmas season in the Netherlands and Belgium, begins on Saint Nicholas (*Sinter Klaas*) Eve, December 5. Special cakes (*letterbanket*) are made in the shape of initials and there are treasure hunts for gifts from Saint Nicholas. On December 6, he rides a white horse through town, dressed in red bishop's robes and is attended by Black Peter, his servant, who keeps a list of the children's good and bad deeds.

Pyrohi

Ukrainian dumplings with savory potato fillings.

2 cups	flour	500 mL
1 tsp.	salt	5 mL
1	egg	1
1 tbsp.	oil OR melted margarine	15 mL
½ cup	warm water (approximately)	125 mL
	or enough to make a soft dough	

In a large bowl, combine the flour, salt and add the egg, oil or melted margarine and enough water to make a soft dough. Knead lightly. Roll out ½ of the dough at a time on a floured board. Cut rounds 2½-3" (6-8 cm) in diameter. Place a round of dough in your palm; add a spoonful of filling (recipe follows); fold dough into a half-circle. Press edges together to seal, frequently dipping fingers into flour to avoid sticking. Lay pyrohi on lightly floured surface (tea towel), cover to prevent drying. **At this point pyrohi may be be frozen.** Place in a single layer on a cookie sheet and freeze. When frozen; place in plastic bags and return to freezer. To cook immediately, prepare a large pot of boiling salted water. Gently lower pyrohi into water; stir with wooden spoon. Boil 5-8 minutes, or until pyrohi float to surface of water. Remove with slotted spoon; rinse quickly with cool water. Prepare melted butter (with sautéed onions, or crisp bacon optional) and coat pyrohi so they do not stick together. Keep warm in oven. Serve with sour cream. Reheat by frying lightly.

Potato Cheese Filling:

2 cups	cooked, mashed potatoes	500 mL
½ cup	grated Cheddar cheese OR more to taste	125 mL
	salt and pepper to taste	

In a large bowl combine all ingredients and use as above.

Potato and Onion Filling:

1	onion, finely chopped	1
2 tbsp.	butter OR margarine	30 mL
2 cups	cooked, mashed potatoes	500 mL
	salt and pepper to taste	

In a skillet, sauté finely chopped onion in butter; remove from heat and add to the mashed potatoes. Add salt and pepper to taste. Use as above.

Sour Cabbage Rolls

This traditional family favorite has been handed down from Mom Mandryk.

2 heads	sour cabbage	2 heads
8 slices	bacon	8 slices
1	onion, chopped	1
3 cups	long-grain rice	750 mL
4¼ cups	cold water	1 L
½ cup	lard OR bacon drippings	125 mL
4 slices	bacon, for topping	4 slices

Onion Cream Sauce:

1	onion, chopped	1
½ cup	butter OR margarine	125 mL
2 cups	whipping cream	500 mL

Wash the sour cabbage in warm water; squeeze gently. This may have to be done 4 or 5 times to remove the brine. Drain on paper towel. Cut out the cabbage core; set aside. Larger leaves may be cut into 2-4 pieces; leave smaller leaves whole. Set aside. To prepare filling, in a large frying pan, combine the bacon and onion and fry over medium heat until onions are just tender; set aside. In a large saucepan, combine the rice, water and lard. Over medium heat, cook for about 10 minutes. Add bacon and onion mixture and cook until the mixture just holds together; about another 10 minutes. Set aside to cool for 20-30 minutes.

To assemble, in a large heavy pan or small roaster, line the bottom and sides with waxed paper, then place a layer of cabbage cores on the pan bottom to prevent the cabbage rolls from burning. Take a cabbage leaf in hand, add about a tablespoon (15 mL) of filling and roll, tucking in the ends. Place rolls in rows in the pan; continuing until all filling and cabbage is used. Place strips of bacon on top. Cover and place in 275°F (140°C) oven.

To prepare sauce, in a large frying pan, cook onion in butter over low heat for 5-8 minutes. Add cream slowly; increase heat to high. Cook on high heat for about 8 minutes, until thickened slightly. Pour over cabbage rolls after they have cooked for about 1 hour. Continue cooking for 4-5 hours, until cabbage is tender.

Makes approximately 100 cabbage rolls

Roast Turkey with Mushroom Bread Stuffing

For variations, try either of the two meat stuffings on the following pages.

12-16 lb.	turkey	**5.5-7 kg**

Mushroom Bread Stuffing:

18 slices	day-old bread, cubed	**18 slices**
¼ cup	butter OR margarine, melted	**60 mL**
3 cups	diced celery	**750 mL**
1	onion, chopped	**1**
10 oz.	can sliced mushrooms, undrained	**284 mL**
1	egg	**1**
1-2 tsp.	poultry seasoning	**5-10 mL**
	salt and pepper to taste	
¼-½ cup	milk to moisten	**60-125 mL**

Thaw the turkey if it is frozen. See **Turkey Tips** on page 135.

To prepare the stuffing, cube the bread, place in a large bowl and set aside. In a skillet over medium heat, melt butter and cook the celery and onions until tender, about 10 minutes. Add to bread cubes and stir to combine. Add mushrooms and liquid, egg, poultry seasoning and salt and pepper. Stir until thoroughly mixed. Add milk to moisten and stir well. Mixture should be quite moist. Stuff turkey just before putting in oven. Preheat oven to 325°F (160°C).

Remove giblets and neck from inside turkey. Rinse bird well with running cold water. Drain well. Spoon some stuffing lightly into neck cavity (do not pack). Fold neck skin over and fasten to back with 1 or 2 skewers. With bird breast side up, lift wings up toward neck, then fold under back of bird so they stay flat and keep neck skin in place. Spoon remaining stuffing into body cavity. Close by folding skin lightly over opening; use skewers to close. Tie legs to tail. Place bird, breast up, on a rack in an open roasting pan. Brush skin all over with vegetable oil or melted butter or margarine. Roast for 4-4½ hours. Baste bird with pan drippings about every hour.

When turkey is cooked, remove it from the oven, loosely tent in foil and allow it to rest for about 20 minutes for easier carving.

Serves 8-12 with leftovers

Pictured on page 137.

Sausage Stuffing

6-8 cups	bread crumbs	1.5-2 L
2 cups	chopped celery	500 mL
1	onion, chopped	1
10 oz.	can sliced mushrooms	284 mL
1 lb.	sausage meat	500 g
1-2 tsp.	poultry seasoning	5-10 mL
	salt and pepper to taste	
¼ cup	butter OR margarine, melted	60 mL
3-4 tbsp.	milk	45-60 mL

In a large bowl, combine the bread crumbs, celery, onions and mush-rooms. Mix thoroughly to combine. Add the sausage and seasonings and work well into the bread crumb mixture. Add the melted butter. Dressing should be quite moist; if it feels dry add 3-4 tbsp.(45-60 mL) of milk. Stuff turkey or bake stuffing in a covered pan at 350°F (180°C) for 1½-2 hours.

Makes stuffing for a 12-15 lb. (5.5-6.5 kg) bird

Herbed Ground Beef Stuffing

1	onion, chopped	1
1 lb.	uncooked lean ground beef	500 g
1 tbsp.	parsley flakes	15 mL
1 tsp.	savory	5 mL
¾ tsp.	salt	3 mL
¼ tsp.	pepper	1 mL
2 tsp.	poultry seasoning	10 mL
½ tsp.	dried thyme	2 mL
5 cups	dried bread crumbs	1.25 L

Chop onion and mix in a large bowl with hamburger. Add parsley flakes, savory, salt, pepper, poultry seasoning and thyme. Mix in bread crumbs. Stuff rinsed bird just before putting into the oven.

Makes enough stuffing for a 12-15 lb. (5.5-6.5 kg) bird

Turkey Tips

✎ *Thawing a Turkey:* Keep frozen turkey in the original plastic wrapping. In the refrigerator it takes about 5 hours per lb. (10 hours per kg) to thaw. Covered with cold water, it takes about 1 hour per lb. (about 2 hours per kg). Change the water several times.

✎ *Approximate Turkey Stuffing Amounts:* For a 12-16 lb. (5.5-7 kg) turkey – about 7 cups (1.75 L) of stuffing, 2 in the neck; 5 in the body cavity.

✎ *Approximate Turkey Roasting Times:* Use a meat thermometer for best results. Time is about 20 minutes per 1 lb. (500 g), to 185°F (85°C) on thermometer inserted into thickest part of thigh. Larger birds need a few minutes per lb. less; smaller birds need a few minutes per lb. more. For stuffed turkey, approximate times at 325°F (160°C) are: 10 lbs. (4.5 kg) – 3½ hours; 12 lbs. (5.5 kg) – 4 hours; 16 lbs. (7 kg) – 5½ hours; 18 lbs. (8 kg) – 5¾-6 hours. Check for doneness ¾-½ hour before set time, to avoid over cooking.

Tempting Turkey Leftovers

Spicy Turkey Chili: Combine sautéed green pepper and onion with cubed turkey, chopped canned tomatoes, canned red kidney beans. Add chili powder and crushed red pepper to taste. Top with nacho or corn chips.

Turkey Grape Salad: Combine cubed turkey, halved green grapes, toasted sliced almonds, chopped green onions, grated orange peel and mayonnaise. Serve on crisp lettuce leaves if you wish. Orange and/or strawberry slices are colorful and tasty additions to this salad.

Turkey Broccoli Stir-Fry: Stir turkey into stir-fried broccoli florets and green or red pepper strips, cauliflower florets and carrot slices, (optional). Add crushed garlic, minced fresh ginger, soy sauce and a sprinkle of sesame oil.

Creamy Turkey and Spinach Tetrazzini: Combine turkey with cooked spaghetti or linguine, chopped sun-dried tomatoes, a pkg. of thawed frozen creamed spinach and crushed garlic. Put in an ovenproof casserole; sprinkle with Parmesan cheese. Bake at 350°F (180°C) until heated through .

Cheesy Turkey Bruschetta: Brush Italian bread slices with olive oil, top with minced garlic; toast in the oven. Combine chopped turkey, shredded mozzarella and chopped fresh basil; spoon on toast slices. Broil to melt cheese.

Roast Christmas Goose

Bohemian Roast Goose

9-11 lb.	frozen goose, thawed	4-5 kg
4 cups	sauerkraut (approximately 2 x 16 oz. [500 g] cans)	1 L
2 cups	peeled, cubed apples	500 mL
1 tsp.	salt	5 mL
½ tsp.	caraway seed	2 mL

Remove giblets and neck from goose; rinse goose well under cold running water. With a two-tined fork, prick skin in several places. In a large bowl, toss sauerkraut with apples, salt and caraway seed; lightly spoon into goose. Skewer neck skin to back. Tie legs and tail together. Lift wings toward neck and fold under back. Place goose, breast up, on a rack in an open roasting pan. Roast at 350°F (180°C) for 4-4½ hours, or until thigh is tender when pierced. Place goose on a warm platter and allow to stand at room temperature 15 minutes before carving. The following fruit stuffing is a good alternative stuffing for goose.

Mixed Fruit Stuffing

12 oz.	pkg. mixed dried fruit, cut into pieces	340 g
2¼ cups	water	550 mL
1	medium onion, minced	1
16 oz.	pkg. fresh cranberries	500 g
1 cup	sugar	250 mL
5 cups	lightly packed, day-old bread cubes	1.25 L
1 tsp.	salt	5 mL
½ tsp.	allspice	2 mL

If prunes in mixed fruit have pits, remove and discard. In a large saucepan over high heat, heat 2 cups (500 mL) water, fruit and onion; bring to a boil. Reduce heat to low; simmer 15 minutes, until fruit is tender; pour mixture into a large bowl. In the same saucepan over medium heat, heat ¼ cup (60 mL) water, cranberries and sugar to boiling. Reduce heat to low; simmer 7 minutes, or until berries pop, stirring occasionally. Drain liquid from berries. Pour berries into fruit mixture. Add the bread cubes, salt and allspice; toss lightly. Lightly spoon into goose and cook as above.

Yuletide Feasts
(Christmas Dinner)

Roast Turkey with Mushroom Bread Stuffing, page 133
Golden Carrot Ring, page 127
Potatoes Romanoff, page 129
Christmas Cranberry Apple Salad, page 114

Duckling à l'Orange

4-5 lb.	frozen duckling, thawed	1.8-2.2 kg
⅛ tsp.	pepper	0.5 mL
¼ tsp.	salt	1 mL
2	oranges	2
¾ cup	chicken stock	175 mL
2 tsp.	cornstarch	10 mL
¼ tsp.	salt	1 mL
¼ cup	sugar	60 mL
2 tbsp.	brandy	30 mL

Preheat oven to 350°F (180°C). Remove giblets and neck from duckling. Rinse bird well under running cold water; pat dry. Remove excess fat from inside of cavity; cut off and discard neck skin. Cut duckling into quarters; sprinkle with pepper and salt.

Place duck pieces, skin side down, in a 9 x 13" (23 x 33 cm) baking pan. Roast for 1 hour; turn and roast for an additional 45 minutes, or until thickest part of drumstick feels soft when pinched with fingers protected with paper towels.

About 30 minutes before duckling is done, prepare sauce. Into a 1-cup (250 mL) measure, squeeze juice from 1 orange; add enough chicken stock to make 1 cup (250 mL). Stir in cornstarch and ¼ tsp. (1 mL) salt until cornstarch is completely dissolved; set aside.

In a heavy saucepan, over medium heat, heat sugar until melted and a light caramel color, stirring constantly with wooden spoon. Remove from heat and let cool 10 minutes. Add orange juice mixture (sugar will harden). Return to heat; cook 5 minutes more, or until reduced to half and sugar is completely dissolved, stirring constantly. Stir in brandy; keep warm.

Slice remaining orange. Arrange duckling pieces on a warm platter and pour orange sauce over duckling. Garnish with orange slices.

Serves 4

Rock Cornish Hens with Dressing

Rice and Mushroom Dressing:

1 cup	long-grain rice	250 mL
½ cup	butter OR margarine	125 mL
¼ lb.	mushrooms, chopped	125 g
¼ cup	chopped onions	60 mL
½ cup	chopped celery	125 mL
2 tbsp.	chopped green pepper	30 mL
½ tsp.	salt	2 mL
⅛ tsp.	pepper	0.5 mL
4 x 1 lb.	Rock Cornish hens	4 x 500 g
¼ cup	melted butter OR margarine	60 mL
	apple rings and parsley for garnish (optional)	

Prepare rice as label directs; set aside. In a skillet over medium heat, melt ½ cup (125 mL) of butter; cook mushrooms, onions, celery and green pepper until vegetables are fork-tender, about 10 minutes. Add the vegetable mixture to the rice. Stir in salt and pepper and set aside. Preheat oven to 375°F (190°C).

Remove giblets and necks from hens. Rinse and drain hens well. Lightly spoon about ½ cup (125 mL) of rice mixture into each hen. Spoon remainder into a 1-quart (1 L) greased casserole; cover; set aside. Tuck neck skin under wings to secure it. With bird breast side up, lift wings up toward neck, then fold wings under the back of the bird. With string, tie legs and tail of each hen together.

Place hens breast side up in an open roasting pan; brush generously with ¼ cup (60 mL) melted butter; sprinkle lightly with salt. Roast, brushing occasionally with drippings in pan, for 1¼ hours, or until a leg can easily be moved up and down. During the last 30 minutes, bake rice dressing in casserole until hot.

Remove strings from hens. Serve hens on rice dressing. If desired, garnish with apple rings and parsley.

Serves 4

Paella

This treasured recipe from Southern Spain is great for a holiday buffet.

3-3½ lb.	broiler-fryer chicken, cut up	1.5-1.75 kg
4 cups	hot water	1 L
1	EACH medium carrot and onion, peeled	1
1	celery stalk	1
3	parsley sprigs	3
1 tsp.	salt	5 mL
1 lb.	pork sausage, cut in ½" (1.3 cm) slices OR Italian OR Ukrainian OR garlic	500 g
½ cup	finely chopped onion	125 mL
10 oz.	can whole clams, drained, reserve liquid	284 mL
4 cups	chicken stock	1 L
2	garlic cloves, crushed	2
1 cup	tomato sauce	250 mL
2 tsp.	paprika	10 mL
1 cup	frozen peas	250 mL
2 cups	uncooked long-grain rice	500 mL
	salt and pepper to taste	
1½ lbs.	fresh shrimp, shelled and deveined OR ¾ lb. (365 g) frozen	750 g
14 oz.	can artichoke hearts, drained	398 mL
4 oz.	pimientos, diced	115 g
¼ cup	minced parsley	60 mL
	pinch of powdered saffron	

Place chicken, water, carrot, onion, celery, parsley sprigs and the salt in a Dutch oven. Cover and bring to a boil; simmer over low heat about 1 hour, until chicken is fork tender. Remove chicken and strain broth. Cool chicken; remove meat from bones; cut meat into bite-size pieces. Cook sausage in saucepan until lightly browned. Add chopped onion and cook about 5 minutes, until tender. Measure broth from chicken and reserved clam liquid; add chicken stock to make 2 quarts (2 L). Add garlic, tomato sauce, paprika and chicken pieces; cook over low heat 15 minutes. Add remaining ingredients, except clams; cover and cook 30 minutes, stirring occasionally until most of the liquid is absorbed. Stir in clams. Cover and cook 5 minutes longer.

Serves 8

Crown Roast of Pork

Colorful cranberry stuffing adds a festive look to your holiday table.

Cranberry Stuffing for Pork Roast:

1 tbsp.	butter OR margarine	15 mL
1	small onion, chopped	1
3 cups	soft bread cubes	750 mL
14 oz.	can whole berry cranberry sauce	398 mL
½ tsp.	rosemary	2 mL
½ cup	chopped parsley	125 mL
⅓ cup	sliced almonds	75 mL
5-7 lb.	pork crown roast OR 7-10 lb. (3-5 kg) roast	2.5-3 kg

To make stuffing, melt butter in a skillet over medium heat. Add onion and cook until translucent. Add bread cubes and stir-fry about 7 minutes, until golden brown. Add ⅓ of the cranberry sauce and all of the rosemary, parsley and almonds; mix well. Stuff roast. Serve the remaining cranberry sauce with the roast. Recipe may be doubled for a larger roast. This stuffing may also be used for rack or loin pork roasts as well.

Small Roasts – 5 to 7 lbs. (to 3 kg)

 Place roast in roasting pan, bones pointing up. Cover bone tips with small pieces of foil. Fill the cavity with the above stuffing. Roast, uncovered, at 325°F (160°C). For a small roast (under 3 kg), cook for 2-2½ hours.

Serves 8-10

Larger Roasts – 7 to 10 lbs. (over 4 kg)

 For a large roast (over 4 kg), roast before stuffing, uncovered, at 325°F (160°C) for 1½ hours. Remove from oven. Drain off excess fat, then fill the cavity with stuffing. Roast for another 2½-3 hours.

To serve, remove roast from oven. Let stand 15 minutes for easier carving. If desired, a paper frill may be placed on each rib.

Serves 15-20

Tourtière

A delicately spiced pork pie, Tourtière is served by French Canadians after Christmas Eve midnight mass. This time is called Réveillon; a time when families gather to rekindle traditions of music, storytelling and feasting.

2 lbs.	lean shoulder pork, finely chopped	1 kg
1 cup	water	250 mL
1	small onion, chopped	1
1	celery stalk and leaves, chopped	1
1 tsp.	salt	5 mL
¼ tsp.	pepper	1 mL
½ tsp.	nutmeg	2 mL
dash	EACH mace and cayenne pepper	dash
	pastry for 2 double-crust pies	

Do not grind the meat. Place pork in a saucepan with water, onion, celery, seasonings and any bone that was left in the meat; cover and simmer until the meat is tender, about 1 hour, adding water if necessary. The mixture when finished should be thick. Remove the bone; season if necessary; cool. Preheat oven to 425°F (220°C). Prepare pastry and line 2, 8" (20 cm) pie plates or 8 individual pie tins. Fill with the meat mixture; add a top crust. Cut top to let the steam escape. Vents can be cut as Christmas trees and/or pastry scraps can be cut as holly or Christmas trees and attached to top crust by brushing milk on pastry appliqués. Bake for 40 minutes. Remove from the oven; cool on a wire rack. Pies can be wrapped and frozen. Reheat pies at 350°F (180°C) for 30 minutes. Serve hot with Chili Sauce or Rhubarb Sauce, page 144.
Serves 8

Variations:

Traditions and recipes vary, various meats, vegetables and seasonings are used. Some recipes stir in 1 cup (250 mL) of well-seasoned mashed potatoes to each 1 lb. (500 g) of cooked meat. Some use ground pork only, others use a combination of half ground pork and veal or pork and beef. Many recipes include ground savory, 1 crushed garlic clove per 1 lb. (500 g) of meat. Cinnamon and allspice are sometimes used. In some recipes, the meat is browned, fat drained off, and the cooking of the meat is continued in beef stock.

Rhubarb Sauce

This is a favorite old Danish recipe that is especially good with pork.

1 qt.	chopped rhubarb	1 L
2 cups	chopped onions	500 mL
2 cups	vinegar	500 mL
4 cups	brown sugar	1 L
1 tsp.	salt	5 mL
1 tsp.	allspice	5 mL
1 tsp.	cinnamon	5 mL
½ tsp.	pepper	2 mL
⅓ tsp.	cloves	1.5 mL

In a large saucepan, combine all ingredients. Cook over medium heat until onions and rhubarb are tender; lower temperature to low and simmer for approximately 2 hours, or until quite thick, stirring frequently. Remove from heat and immediately pour into sterilized jars.

Makes 2-3, 2-cup (500 mL) containers

Chili Sauce

Tangy homemade chili sauce is superb with roast beef or with any beef or pork dishes.

6 qts.	ripe tomatoes	6 L
4 cups	diced onions	1 L
¼ tsp.	cayenne pepper	1 mL
4 cups	diced celery	1 L
2	large green peppers, diced	2
2	large red peppers, diced	2
½ cup	coarse salt	125 mL
4 cups	white sugar	1 L
2 cups	vinegar	500 mL
2 tbsp.	mustard seed	30 mL
5 tbsp.	pickling spice (in a bag)	75 mL

Chili Sauce

Continued

Remove tomato skins; put tomatoes in a large kettle. Add the onions, cayenne pepper, celery and peppers. Sprinkle with coarse salt. Let stand a few hours or overnight. Add sugar, vinegar, mustard seed and pickling spice. Boil 20 minutes over medium heat, until vegetables are slightly cooked but still crisp. Remove from heat and pour into sterilized jars and seal.

Makes 6-8, 2-cup (500 mL) containers

Creamy Beef Stroganoff

Our tasty version of a traditional stroganoff is a family favorite.

1-1½ lbs.	lean beef, cut in 1½-2" (4-5 cm) cubes	500-750 g
½ lb.	mushrooms	250 g
½ cup	chopped onions	125 mL
3	garlic cloves, minced	3
10 oz.	can tomato soup	284 mL
1 tbsp.	Worcestershire sauce	15 mL
6-8 drops	Tabasco sauce	6-8 drops
½ tsp.	salt	2 mL
⅛ tsp.	pepper	0.5 mL
¾-1 cup	whipping cream	175-250 mL

In large, ovenproof saucepan over medium-high heat, brown the beef cubes. Add all the other ingredients, except the cream. Cover saucepan and bake in the oven at 325°F (160°C) for 1½-2 hours, or simmer on top of the stove for the same amount of time. Remove from oven and add cream slowly, stirring constantly to blend. Return to oven for an additional 20-30 minutes. Do not allow to boil after the cream has been added. Serve with broad egg noodles.

Serves 6-8

Beef Wellington

An old English tradition, this delicious dish is sure to be a crowd pleaser.

4 lb.	whole beef tenderloin	2 kg
¾ cup	Burgundy	175 mL
¾ cup	dry sherry	175 mL
2	bay leaves	2
1	onion, quartered	1
1 lb.	fresh mushrooms, chopped (3 cups [750 mL])	500 g
½ cup	chopped onion	125 mL
2 tbsp.	butter OR margarine	30 mL
½ cup	liverwurst OR liver pâté	125 mL
¼ cup	fine dry bread crumbs	60 mL
2 cups	flour	500 mL
½ tsp.	salt	2 mL
⅔ cup	shortening	150 mL
⅓-½ cup	cold water	75-125 mL
1	egg, beaten	1
¾ cup	water	175 mL
½ cup	cold water	125 mL
3 tbsp.	flour	45 mL
	salt and pepper to taste	

Place meat in a plastic bag and place bag in a deep bowl. Combine Burgundy, dry sherry, bay leaves and onion. Pour over meat in bag and close. Chill overnight; turn bag occasionally to distribute the marinade.

Next day, remove meat from bag; reserve marinade. Preheat oven to 425°F (220°C). Place meat on a rack in a shallow roasting pan. Roast for 1-1¾ hours (depending on desired taste, 1 hour being quite rare). Remove meat from pan; cool 20 minutes. Reserve drippings. Trim any fat from meat.

While the roast is cooking, cook mushrooms and chopped onions in butter until tender, about 6 minutes. Remove from heat; stir in liverwurst or liver pâté, crumbs, and 3 tbsp. (45 mL) of the reserved marinade. (Save remaining marinade.) Cover; chill at least 1 hour.

Beef Wellington

Continued

To make the pastry, stir together the 2 cups (500 mL) of flour and ½ tsp. (2 mL) salt. Cut in shortening until size of small peas. Gradually add ⅓-½ cup (75-125 mL) cold water, 1 tbsp. (15 mL) at a time, tossing with fork until all is moistened. Form into a ball. Preheat oven to 425°F (220°C).

On a floured surface, roll dough to a 12 x 14" (30 x 35 cm) rectangle. Spread mushroom and onion mixture to within 1" (2.5 cm) of edges. Center meat on top. Wrap pastry around meat; bringing pastry over meat on both long sides. Overlap long sides. Brush edges with egg and seal. Trim excess pastry from ends; fold up. Brush with egg and seal. Place roast, seam down, on a greased baking sheet. Brush egg over all. Reroll pastry trimmings. Cut into strips; criss-cross over pastry case to give a decorative look. Brush with remaining egg.

Bake until pastry is golden, 30-35 minutes. Heat ¾ cup (175 mL) water with reserved drippings until solids dissolve. Mix ½ cup (125 mL) cold water with 3 tbsp. (45 mL) flour; stir into drippings with ¼ cup (60 mL) reserved marinade. Cook and stir until bubbly; season with salt and pepper. Serve with the roast.

Serves 12

 # The Christmas Feast

A bountiful table at Christmas harks back to the ancient Romans' orgy of eating during Saturnalia. Feasting probably also stems from the practice of fasting during Advent, the four weeks preceding Christmas. In medieval England, the Christmas feast was ushered in with a boar's head, which was ceremoniously brought to the table and celebrated in song before the guests dined on such delicacies as roast venison, boar, mutton and peacock. Most modest feasts featured roast goose, which has since been supplanted by the now traditional roast turkey. Spices are important ingredients in such Christmas dishes as plum pudding and gingerbread. The use of exotic seasonings carries on the medieval custom of preparing Christmas pies with spices brought from the East, the Christ Child's birthplace.

Smoked Salmon Lasagna

*Smoked salmon and dill give a special occasion flavor
to this superb buffet or dinner dish.*

6	lasagna noodles	6
2 tbsp.	olive oil	30 mL

Sherried Cream Sauce:

¼ cup	butter OR margarine	60 mL
½ cup	finely chopped onion	125 mL
¼ cup	flour	60 mL
2 cups	chicken stock	500 mL
¼ cup	half and half cereal cream	60 mL
2 tbsp.	dry sherry	30 mL
pinch	cayenne pepper	pinch
1	egg yolk beaten	1

Smoked Salmon Filling:

2 cups	well-drained ricotta cheese	500 mL
2	eggs, lightly beaten	2
2 tbsp.	chopped fresh dill	30 mL
½	lemon, juice and grated peel of	½
¾ lb.	sliced smoked salmon	365 g
16 oz.	mozzarella cheese slices	500 g
1 cup	Parmesan cheese	250 mL

Boil noodles as per package directions; drain and toss with oil. Spread on waxed paper.

To make the sauce, melt butter over medium-low heat in a medium frying pan. Add onion and sauté until soft, about 5 minutes. Add flour, stirring constantly, and allow to bubble for 1-2 minutes. Whisk in the chicken stock and then the cream. Stir in the sherry and cayenne pepper; cook, stirring constantly, for 6-8 minutes, until the mixture thickens. Remove from heat and whisk in the egg yolk.

To make the filling, in a bowl combine the ricotta cheese, beaten eggs, dill and lemon juice and peel. Mix well.

Smoked Salmon Lasagna

Continued

Assemble in a 9 x 13" (13 x 23 cm) baking pan. Spread ¼ cup (60 mL) of sauce on the bottom. Place 3 noodles over top; spread with ½ of the ricotta cheese; then ½ of the smoked salmon slices; then ½ of the mozzarella cheese slices. Pour 1 cup (250 mL) of the sauce over the cheese; spread evenly; layer 3 more noodles, repeat the layering. Sprinkle with Parmesan cheese. Bake at 350°F (180°C) for 50-60 minutes. Serves 8

Coquilles St. Jacques

1 lb.	scallops, cut into quarters	500 g
½ lb.	cooked, peeled shrimp, cut up	250 g
1	medium onion, finely chopped	1
1 cup	white wine	250 mL
½ lb.	mushrooms, sliced	250 g
½ cup	water	125 mL
1 tbsp.	lemon juice	15 mL
¼ cup	EACH butter OR margarine, flour	60 mL
1 cup	half and half cereal cream	250 mL
2	egg yolks, beaten	2
	salt and pepper to taste	
1 cup	bread crumbs	250 mL
½ cup	grated Parmesan cheese	125 mL
¼ cup	butter OR margarine, melted	60 mL

Preheat oven to 400°F (200°C). Cook scallops, shrimp and onion in wine for about 5 minutes. Drain; reserve liquid. Cook mushrooms in water with lemon juice for about 8 minutes. Drain; reserve juice. Melt ¼ cup (60 mL) butter; add flour and, stirring constantly, cook to a smooth paste. Remove from heat; add cream, stirring constantly. Add some sauce to beaten eggs; return to sauce; blend well. Over low heat, add reserved wine, mushroom liquid, stir until smooth and thick. Add salt and pepper, scallops, shrimp, onions and mushrooms. Blend well, heat gently; pour into a shallow 9" square (23 cm) baking dish. Sprinkle with bread crumbs and cheese; drizzle with ¼ cup (60 mL) melted butter. Cook for 20-30 minutes, or until top is nicely brown.

Serves 6

Creamy Dilled Seafood Casserole

This rich, delicious combination of seafood is served in a delicate dill sauce.

3 tbsp.	butter	45 mL
1 cup	chopped onion	250 mL
4	garlic cloves, minced	4
2	medium carrots, cut in julienne	2
1½ cups	finely chopped celery	375 mL
1 lb.	fresh scallops	500 g
1 lb.	cooked shrimp with tails on	500 g
½ lb.	cooked crab meat, coarsely chopped	250 g
3 tbsp.	flour	45 mL
1½ cups	milk	375 mL
8 oz.	cream cheese	250 g
2 tbsp.	chopped fresh dillweed OR 1½ tsp. (7 mL) dried	30 mL
1 tsp.	salt	5 mL
1 tsp.	pepper	5 mL
1½ cups	crushed seasoned croûtons	375 mL
2 tbsp.	melted butter	30 mL

In a large skillet, melt 1 tbsp. (15 mL) of butter over medium heat. Cook onion, garlic, carrots and celery until tender, stirring occasionally. Set aside. In a large skillet, in 3 cups (750 mL) of simmering water, poach scallops until opaque, approximately 1-2 minutes. Remove scallops with slotted spoon; place in a large bowl. Reserve 1 cup (250 mL) of poaching liquid. Add the whole cooked shrimp and crab meat to scallops.

To make the sauce, in a skillet, melt 2 tbsp. (30 mL) of butter over medium heat; whisk in flour and the reserved poaching liquid and milk. Cook, stirring until sauce thickens. Whisk in cream cheese, stirring until cheese melts, then add dill, salt and pepper. Stir into the seafood mixture. Butter a 9 x 13" (23 x 33 cm) casserole and pour in seafood mixture. At this point, casserole may be cooled, covered and refrigerated overnight or frozen for up to 2 weeks; then thawed in the refrigerator. Preheat oven to 325°F (160°C). Combine crushed croûtons with melted butter and sprinkle over casserole. Bake 45-50 minutes. Delicious served over rice or noodles or as part of a buffet.

Serves 8

Perfect Baked Ham

Glaze variations provide delicious variety to this splendid holiday buffet main-course dish.

| 12-15 lb. | fully cooked ham | 5.5-6.5 kg |

Brown Sugar and Mustard Glaze:

1 cup	brown sugar	250 mL
2 tbsp.	flour	30 mL
1 tbsp.	dry mustard	15 mL
	enough vinegar to make a thin paste.	
½ cup	corn syrup OR honey	125 mL

Preheat oven to 350°F (180°C). Place ham on a rack in an open roasting pan. Bake for 2 hours. While ham is baking, prepare glaze. Combine brown sugar, flour and mustard with enough vinegar to make a thick paste. Remove pan from oven and increase temperature to 450°F (230°C). Cut ham and peel off all skin. Using a sharp knife, score fat by cutting about ¼" (1 cm) deep in 1-1½" (2.5-4 cm) diamonds. Brush ham surface with the corn syrup or honey. Then spread the glaze over the entire surface. If desired, fasten maraschino cherries and pineapple slices to the ham with toothpicks. Return to oven for 10-15 minutes. Baste frequently with the glaze that drips into the pan. Remove from oven and continue to baste with syrup for 10 minutes. Glaze should be firm enough at the end of this time to hold cherries and pineapple without the toothpicks.

This recipe makes enough glaze for a whole ham. The glaze may be used on half hams, cottage rolls, etc. Reduce quantities depending on the size of the ham.

Variations:

Try either the Orange Glaze or the Pineapple Glaze on the next page in place of the Brown Sugar and Mustard Glaze.

Orange Glaze

1 cup	orange marmalade	250 mL
1 tbsp.	prepared mustard	15 mL
1	small orange	1
	whole cloves	

Bake ham as on page 151. To prepare orange glaze, in a small saucepan over low heat, heat orange marmalade and mustard until marmalade is melted. When the ham is cooked, remove ham from oven and score as on page 151. With a brush, brush half of the prepared orange glaze evenly over the entire surface of the ham. Return to oven and bake for an additional 10-15 minutes. Remove from oven. Cut orange in very thin slices and halve slices; arrange in rows over the ham, overlapping them slightly and fastening with whole cloves. Brush remaining warm glaze over the orange slices. Return ham to oven and bake 10 minutes more, until the orange slices are heated through.

Makes enough glaze for a whole ham.

Pineapple Glaze

| 10 oz. | can crushed pineapple, drained | 284 mL |
| ½ cup | brown sugar, packed | 125 mL |

Bake ham as on page 151. To prepare glaze, in a bowl combine the crushed pineapple with the sugar. When the ham is cooked, remove ham from oven and score as on page 151. With a spoon, evenly pat the prepared pineapple mixture over the ham. Return ham to oven and bake for an additional 20 minutes.

Makes enough glaze for a whole ham

Sweet Endings

Desserts

Apple Bread Pudding with Maple Rum Sauce

This old-fashioned recipe is the ultimate in comfort food. Maple Rum Sauce adds a modern sophistication to a childhood favorite.

4 cups	day-old French bread cubes	1 L
2 cups	pared, cored, chopped apples	500 mL
½ cup	washed, dried raisins	125 mL
3	eggs	3
10 oz.	can sweetened condensed milk	284 mL
1¾ cups	hot water	425 mL
¼ cup	butter OR margarine, melted	60 mL
1 tsp.	maple extract	5 mL

In a large bowl, combine bread crumbs, apples and raisins. Place in a greased 9" (23 cm) square baking pan. In a large bowl, beat eggs, stir in sweetened condensed milk, water, butter and maple extract. Pour over bread cube mixture, completely moistening bread. Bake at 350°F (180°C) for 45-50 minutes, or until a knife inserted in the center comes out clean. Cool slightly. Serve warm with Maple Rum Sauce, below.

Serves 8

Maple Rum Sauce:

¼ cup	butter OR margarine, melted	60 mL
1 cup	packed brown sugar	250 mL
½ cup	whipping cream	125 mL
2 tbsp.	rum	30 mL
½ tsp.	maple extract	2 mL

In a medium saucepan, melt butter; stir in brown sugar and whipping cream. Over medium heat, cook and stir until mixture comes to a boil. Boil 2-3 minutes. Remove from heat; stir in rum and maple extract. Cool slightly.

Makes 1½ cups (375 mL)

Variation:

To make **Vanilla Brandy Sauce**, substitute vanilla for the maple extract and substitute brandy for the rum.

Sweet Endings
(Desserts)

Holiday Trifle, page 162
Mandarin Chocolate Cheesecake, page 158

Almond Cheesecake

The delicate almond flavor combines with the rich chocolate crust to create a superb ending to any yuletide feast.

Chocolate Crumb Crust:

2½ cups	chocolate wafer crumbs	625 mL
⅓ cup	sugar	75 mL
6 tbsp.	softened butter	90 mL

Creamy Amaretto Filling:

3 x 8 oz.	cream cheese, softened	3 x 250 g
1 cup	sugar	250 mL
5	eggs	5
⅓ cup	whipping cream	75 mL
¼ cup	amaretto	60 mL

Sour Cream Amaretto Topping:*

1 cup	sour cream	250 mL
1 tbsp.	sugar	15 mL
1 tbsp.	amaretto	15 mL
	sliced almonds	

Combine the crust ingredients in a bowl. Mix well. Pat over the bottom of a 12" (30 cm) springform pan.

To make the filling, in a large mixing bowl, with an electric mixer, beat together the softened cream cheese and sugar. Beat in eggs, one at a time, beating well after each addition. Add the whipping cream and amaretto and beat until light. Pour over the crust and bake at 350°F (180°C) for 50-60 minutes. Remove from oven and let stand 5 minutes. (Cake will not be quite set.)

Combine all the topping ingredients except the sliced almonds. Spread over hot cake and sprinkle sliced almonds over all. Return to the oven for 5 minutes. Remove from the oven and cool on a wire rack. Store in the refrigerator at least a day before serving. If you wish you can drizzle melted chocolate over the top for a more sumptuous effect.

Serves 18-20

* Any topping may be used in place of the sour cream topping.

Mandarin Chocolate Cheesecake

This fabulous creamy cheesecake, decorated with mandarin segments and chocolate curls, is truly a dessert made in heaven.

Chocolate Crumb Crust:

1 cup	chocolate wafer crumbs	250 mL
3 tbsp.	butter OR margarine, melted	45 mL

Triple Orange Filling:

3 x 8 oz.	cream cheese, softened	3 x 250 g
¾ cup	sugar	175 mL
3 tbsp.	flour	45 mL
3	eggs	3
¼ cup	orange juice	60 mL
3 tbsp.	orange liqueur	45 mL
1 tbsp.	grated orange rind	15 mL

Ganache Glaze and Decoration:

½ cup	whipping cream	125 mL
4 x 1 oz.	squares semisweet chocolate, chopped	4 x 30 g
10 oz.	can mandarin orange segments	284 mL
2 x 1 oz.	squares semisweet chocolate chocolate curls (optional)	2 x 30 g

To make the crust, combine the wafers and melted butter. Press over the bottom of a 9" (23 cm) springform pan. Bake at 325°F (160°C) for 10 minutes.

To make the filling, in a large bowl, beat cream cheese, sugar and flour until smooth. Beat in eggs, one at a time, just until blended. Mix in juice, liqueur and rind. Pour over prepared crust and bake at 350°F (180°C) for 45 minutes, or until center is just set. Remove from oven. Cool thoroughly on wire rack. Remove pan rim and chill overnight.

To make the glaze, bring cream to a boil over low heat, remove from heat. Stir in the chopped chocolate until melted and smooth. Pour over cake.

Mandarin Chocolate Cheesecake

Continued

Lay mandarin orange segments out on a paper towel and let dry thoroughly. Partially melt 2 squares of semisweet chocolate over hot water. Remove from heat and continue stirring until completely melted. Then take each mandarin orange segment and, after dipping one end into the melted chocolate, place them all on waxed paper. Refrigerate until chocolate has hardened. Arrange in a circle on the cake. If desired, pile chocolate curls, see instructions below, in the center of the cake.

Serves 12-15

Pictured on page 155.

Chocolate Curls

1. Dip a vegetable peeler into boiling water and dry well. For wide curls, slowly and firmly pull warm vegetable peeler across the wide side of a square of unsweetened or semisweet chocolate. Use the thin side of the chocolate for thin curls. Or you can use the shredder side of a box grater to make curly shreds. Shred onto waxed paper.

2. Warm chocolate by heating in the microwave on high for 30 seconds, 1 oz. (30 g) at a time or hand hold wrapped squares about 1 minute, or until slightly softened. Proceed as above with cold vegetable peeler. Curls may be used to garnish frosted cakes, cheesecakes, pies or whipped-cream desserts. 5-6, 1 oz. (30 g) squares will cover a 9" (23 cm) cake. Refrigerate curls on a plate or tray until ready to use.

3. To make very large curls or ripples of chocolate, spread melted chocolate evenly over a baking sheet. Chill in refrigerator for about 5 minutes, until set. If chocolate is too hard, let it sit at room temperature for a few minutes. For medium curls, pull the side of a spoon bowl towards you through the chocolate. To make large curls, use a knife or scraper. Scrape chocolate away from you.

White Chocolate Strawberry Mousse Cake

Fresh strawberries and white chocolate create a lavish presentation for Christmas or any season.

Vanilla Almond Crumb Crust:

1 cup	vanilla wafer crumbs	250 mL
½ cup	toasted almonds, finely chopped	125 mL
¼ cup	melted butter	60 mL

White Chocolate Strawberry Filling:

12 x 1 oz.	squares white chocolate	12 x 30 g
1 cup	cubed sponge cake	250 mL
4 cups	fresh strawberries, hulled	1 L
4 oz.	cream cheese, softened	125 g
¼ cup	sugar	60 mL
¼ cup	orange liqueur OR frozen concentrated orange juice	60 mL
1 tsp.	vanilla	5 mL
2 cups	whipping cream, whipped	500 mL

Combine vanilla wafer crumbs, almonds and butter. Press into the bottom of a 9" (23 cm) springform pan. Melt chocolate over hot water. Drizzle or carefully spread 3 tbsp. (45 mL) of chocolate over the vanilla wafer base. Cut sponge cake into small cubes and sprinkle over the chocolate in the pan. Reserve 12 strawberries for garnish and arrange the remaining whole berries, point up, on top of the sponge cake cubes.

Beat cream cheese until smooth and beat in sugar. Mix in orange liqueur or orange juice and vanilla. Beat in remaining cooled chocolate. Gradually fold in the whipped cream and pour over the strawberries in pan. Garnish the top with the 12 saved strawberries. Cover and chill for 4-6 hours.

Serves 12-14

Tiramisu

This rich Italian trifle is a combination of Italian cream cheese, whipping cream, coffee and liqueur – a sensational dessert.

3	egg yolks	3
½ cup	sugar	125 mL
⅓ cup	Tia Maria OR Kahlúa liqueur	75 mL
½ lb.	Mascarpone cheese*	250 g
1 cup	whipping cream	250 mL
1 cup	extra strong coffee, cold	250 mL
⅓ cup	Tia Maria OR Kahlúa liqueur	75 mL
24	large Italian ladyfingers	24
¾ cup	semisweet chocolate, finely chopped	175 mL

Beat egg yolks with sugar until light. Beat in ⅓ cup (75 mL) of liqueur. Cook gently in a double boiler or in a stainless steel or glass bowl set over a pot of simmering water. Stir constantly, until thickened. Mixture should be thick and creamy. Remove from heat and cool. Beat mascarpone cheese until smooth and then slowly beat in cooled custard. Whip cream until stiff and gently fold into the cheese mixture. Set aside. Combine coffee with ⅓ cup (75 mL) of liqueur and set aside. Line a 9" (23 cm) square baking dish or a trifle bowl with ladyfingers. Brush ladyfingers with half of the coffee mixture. Spread with half of the cheese filling mixture. Sprinkle with half of the chopped chocolate. Repeat layers, starting with ladyfingers; brush with coffee mixture, spreading remaining filling over ladyfingers and topping with chocolate. Remember to completely cover ladyfingers with cheese mixture. Cover and refrigerate 6-8 hours or overnight.

Serves 10-12

Note:

Tiramisu may be frozen for up to 1 month. Defrost in refrigerator for several hours before serving.

* Mascarpone is a buttery rich Italian cream cheese, it is very expensive and may be difficult to find. To substitute for Mascarpone, use 8 oz. (250 g) of cream cheese and beat in 1 tbsp. (15 mL) of butter and ¼ cup (60 mL) of sour cream.

Holiday Trifle

5 oz.	pkg. vanilla pudding and pie filling (6-serving size), not instant	135 g
3 cups	milk	750 mL
6 x 1 oz.	squares white chocolate, chopped	6 x 30 g
2 cups	whipping cream, whipped	500 mL
½	pound cake, cubed	½
¼ cup	orange liqueur OR orange juice	60 mL
2½ cups	sliced, sweetened fresh OR frozen strawberries	625 mL
5 x 1 oz.	squares white chocolate, grated	5 x 30 g
6-8	whole strawberries, for garnish	6-8
1 oz.	square white chocolate, melted, cooled	30 g

Prepare pudding according to package directions with milk. Remove from heat; stir in the 6 squares of chocolate until melted and smooth. Cover and chill. Fold in 1 cup (250 mL) of whipped cream. Drizzle cake with liqueur. In the bottom of a deep glass bowl, layer half the cake cubes, half the berries, half the pudding and half the grated chocolate. Repeat layers, ending with chocolate. Top with whipped cream. Garnish with berries, drizzle with melted chocolate. Chill.
Serves 8
Pictured on page 155.

Baked Alaska

2 cups	sifted cake flour	500 mL
2 tsp.	baking powder	10 mL
1 tsp.	salt	5 mL
⅓ cup	butter OR margarine	75 mL
1¼ cups	sugar	300 mL
5	eggs separated	5
½ cup	milk	125 mL
1 tsp.	vanilla	5 mL
2 qt.	block of vanilla ice cream	2 L
dash	cream of tartar	dash
¾ cup	berry sugar	175 mL
	Cherries Jubilee (recipe follows)	

Baked Alaska

Continued

Preheat oven to 350°F (180°C). Sift together flour, baking powder and salt onto waxed paper. Beat butter and sugar in a large bowl at high speed until light and fluffy. Beat in egg yolks, one at a time, until well blended. Stir in flour mixture alternately with milk and vanilla, beating well after each addition until batter is smooth. Spread batter into a greased, floured 9" (23 cm) baking pan. Bake for 40 minutes, until top springs back when lightly touched. Cool in a pan on a wire rack for 10 minutes; remove from pan and cool completely on wire rack.

Place cake on a small cookie sheet; unmold block of ice cream onto center of cake. Freeze cake and ice cream while beating egg whites. Beat egg whites and cream of tartar until foamy in a large bowl with mixer at high speed. Beat in berry sugar, 1 tbsp. (15 mL) at a time, until meringue forms firm peaks. Spread meringue over ice cream and cake to coat completely, making deep swirls on top with spatula. Freeze until meringue is firm, then cover with plastic wrap. Meringue-covered cake can be frozen up to 1 week.

To cook, brown in preheated 425°F (220°C) oven for 5 minutes, or just until peaks turn golden. Slide onto a serving platter; serve immediately with Cherries Jubilee, below. Freeze any remaining dessert.

Serves 12-15

Cherries Jubilee

19 oz.	can sweet dark cherries	540 mL
	water	
¼ cup	sugar	60 mL
2 tbsp.	cornstarch	30 mL
¼ cup	brandy OR rum	60 mL

Drain syrup from cherries into a 2-cup (500 mL) measure. Add water to make 2 cups (500 mL). Combine sugar and cornstarch in a large heavy saucepan; stir in cherry liquid. Cook, stirring constantly, until sauce thickens and bubbles, approximately 1 minute. Stir in cherries and brandy or rum. Simmer 5 minutes. Serve hot. Sauce can be made ahead; cool, then refrigerate. Reheat before serving. Makes 4 cups (1 L)

Holiday Menu Suggestions

Christmas Eve

Rich Brandied Eggnog, page 98
Mistletoe Punch, page 100
French Onion Soup, page 111
Beef Wellington, page 146
Potatoes Romanoff, page 129
Crunchy Broccoli, page 121
Corn Mushroom Bake, page 126
Holiday Trifle, page 162
Amaretto Fruit Cake, page 30
Holiday Spritz Cookies, page 39

Ukrainian Christmas Eve (Contemporary)

Rich Brandied Eggnog, page 98
Mistletoe Punch, page 100
Christmas Sauerkraut Soup, page 110
Pyrohi, page 131
Sour Cabbage Rolls, page 132
Smoked Salmon Lasagna, page 148
Creamy Dilled Seafood Casserole, page 150
Golden Carrot Ring (fill center with green beans), page 127
Christmas Cranberry Apple Salad, page 114
Light Coconut Fruit Cake, page 32
Coconut Almond Tarts, page 67; Butter Tarts, page 68

Christmas Morning Brunch

Christmas Morning Punch, page 98
Overnight Wine and Cheese Omelet, page 80
Shrimp and Corn Salad, page 120
Cashew and Orange Salad, page 118
Orangeberry Muffins, page 92
Christmas Pull Aparts, page 84
Hot Cappuccino Punch, page 97

Christmas Dinner (1)

Mistletoe Punch, page 100
Sherried Mushroom Soup, page 112
Roast Turkey with Mushroom Bread Stuffing, page 133
Whipped Potato Casserole, page 130
Green Vegetable Medley, page 122
Holiday Turnips, page 128
Cranberry Sparkle Salad, page 114
Mom's Steamed Carrot Christmas Pudding, page 27
Caramel Sauce, page 28
Mom's Traditional Christmas Cake, page 35
Brown Sugar Shortbread Wedges, page 49

Christmas Dinner (2)

Golden Glow Punch, page 100
Tossed Greens with Raspberry Vinaigrette, page 117
Roast Christmas Goose with Mixed Fruit Stuffing, page 136
Holiday Sweet Potatoes, page 128
Spinach Puff, page 126
Cauliflower with Shrimp Sauce, page 124
Christmas Cranberry Apple Salad, page 114
Traditional Old-Fashioned Scots' Plum Pudding, page 26
Old-Fashioned Orange Sauce, page 28
Traditional Scottish Shortbread, page 48
Dark Fruit Cake, page 34

Boxing Day Brunch

Christmas Morning Punch, page 98
Creamy Eggnog, page 99
Fresh Fruit Salad, page 116
Fantastic Mushroom Three-Cheese Eggs, page 78
(serve with grilled bacon and sausages)
Potato Pancakes, page 73
Piña Colada Muffins, page 92
Apricot Almond Coffee Cake, page 83

New Year's Eve Buffet

Wassail Bowl with Baked Apples, page 96
Christmas Morning Punch, page 98
Paella, page 141
Mexican Crêpes, page 74
Fire and Ice Tomatoes, page 119
Almond Cheesecake, page 157
White Chocolate Strawberry Mousse Cake, page 160

New Year's Eve Dinner

Golden Glow Punch, page 100
Sherried Mushroom Soup, page 112
Crown Roast of Pork, page 142
Rhubarb Sauce, page 144
Whipped Potato Casserole, page 130
The Great Green Vegetable Bake, page 122
Corn-Mushroom Bake, page 126
Baked Alaska, page 162

New Year's Day Dinner

Mistletoe Punch, page 100
Crab Stuffed Mushrooms, page 108
Perfect Baked Ham with Orange Glaze, page 151
Dilled Cheezy Hash Browns, page 75
Cauliflower Tomato Medley, page 125
Green Vegetable Medley, page 122
Golden Glow Salad, page 115
Mandarin Chocolate Cheesecake, page 158

Après Ski or Skating Party

Hot Mulled Wine, page 97
Hot Cappuccino Punch, page 97
Broccoli & Cheese Tarts, page 109
Smoked Salmon Lasagna, page 148
Cashew and Orange Salad, page 118
Apple Bread Pudding with Maple Rum Sauce, page 154

Holiday Open House

APPETIZERS

Rich Brandied Eggnog, page 98
Golden Glow Punch, page 100
Simply Delicious Cheese Ball, page 102
Spinach Dip, page 105
Broccoli and Cheese Tarts, page 109
Oriental Chicken Wings, page 108
Savory Cheesecake Pâté (assorted crackers), page 102

DESSERTS

Mom's Traditional Christmas Cake, page 35
Traditional Scottish Dundee Cake, page 36
Flarn, page 45
Greek Shortbread, page 47
Brown Sugar Shortbread Wedges, page 49
Chocolate-Covered Cherry Cookies, page 57
Rocky Road Fudge Bars, page 60
Caramel Bars, page 64
Lemon Squares, page 66
Mom's Butter Tarts, page 68

Cookie Exchange

Holiday Sugar Cookies, page 40
Gingerbread Cookies, page 42
Kanel Kakor, page 44
Orechove Kolieska Llepovane, page 46
Traditional Scottish Shortbread, page 48
Brown Sugar Shortbread, page 49
Mexican Mocha Balls, page 53
Angel Pillows, page 54
Mom Mandryk's Christmas Nuggets, page 56
Chocolate-Covered Cherry Cookies, page 57
Holiday Hideways, page 58
Christmas Rum Balls, page 12

Index

Appetizers

Broccoli and Cheese Tarts 109
Crab and Cheese Spread 107
Crab-Stuffed Mushrooms................. 108
Crab Swiss Spread 107
Oriental Chicken Wings 108
Savory Cheesecake Pâté 102
Shrimp and Cheese Spread.............. 106
Simply Delicious Cheese Ball 102
Spinach Dip...................................... 105
Spinach Tarts.................................... 109
Tuna Mold 106

Bars, Squares & Tarts

Almond Bars..................................... 65
Butter Tarts, Mom's 68
Caramel Bars.................................... 64
Chocolate Pecan Bars 59
Coconut Almond Tarts..................... 67
Lemon Squares 66
Pastry, Mom's 68
Rocky Road Fudge Bars 60
Shortbread Caramel Fingers............ 63
Turtle Bars.. 62

Beverages

Almond Vanilla Coffee 19
Cappuccino Mix................................ 19
Christmas Morning Punch............... 98
Creamy Eggnog................................ 99
Golden Glow Punch........................ 100
Hot Cappuccino Punch 97
Hot Mulled Wine 97
Mocha Coffee 19
Mistletoe Punch.............................. 100
Orange Cream 99
Pineapple Julius.............................. 100
Rich Brandied Eggnog..................... 98
Wassail Bowl with Baked Apples... 96

Breads & Muffins

Apricot Almond Coffee Cake.......... 83
Cherry Almond Wreath.................... 88
Christmas Pull-Aparts 84
Cranberry Fruit Bread...................... 94
Cranberry Muffins............................ 93
Orangeberry Muffins 92
Panettone.. 87
Piña Colada Muffins 92
Stollen.. 90

Brunch Dishes

Caramel Oven French Toast 70
Christmas Morning Italian Strata ... 81
Mexican Crêpes................................ 74
Crustless Crab Quiche 77
Dilled Cheesy Hash Browns........... 75
Eggs Benedict................................... 79
Fantastic Mushroom Three-
   Cheese Eggs................................. 78
Fluffy Buttermilk Pancakes............. 72
Holiday Brunch Pie 76
Mexican Crêpes................................ 74
Overnight Wine and Cheese
   Omelet 80
Pineapple Pancakes 72
Potato Pancakes................................ 73
Puffed Apple Pancakes 71
Quiche Lorraine 76
Seafood Brunch Bake 82

Cakes

Amaretto Fruit Cake......................... 30
Cherry Bundt Cake........................... 37
Cream Cheese Frosting..................... 39
Dark Fruit Cake................................ 34
Dundee Cake, Traditional Scottish   36
Everyday Fruit Cake 33
Icing Sugar Glaze............................. 37
Light Coconut Fruit Cake................. 32
Old-Fashioned Carrot Cake............. 38
Plum Pudding, Traditional Old-
   Fashioned Scots' 26
Steamed Carrot Christmas
   Pudding, Mom's 27
Traditional Christmas Cake,
   Mom's 35

Candy & Gift-Giving Ideas

Almond Roca..................................... 13
Almond Vanilla Coffee 19
Antipasto 21
Baked Caramel Corn......................... 16
Cappuccino Mix................................ 19
Chocolate Almond Bark 14
Chocolate Hazelnut Apricot Bark .. 14
Chocolate Orange Truffles 11
Chocolate Truffles 10
Christmas Dough Ornaments 24
Christmas Rum Balls........................ 12
Cinnamon Craft Ornaments............ 24
Coconut Candy, Aunt Susie's........... 9
Dilly Dilly Crackers.......................... 15

Dog Bones... 23
Ganache Filling.................................... 10
Hazelnut Truffles 11
Hot Pepper Oil 22
Marbled Bark 14
Marzipan Fruits, Vegetables and
  Figures 7
Marzipan Kartoffel 7
Mocha Coffee....................................... 19
Noël Nuts 15
Nuts and Bolts..................................... 16
Raspberry Vinegar 22
Raspberry Wine Jelly......................... 20
Strawberry Champagne Jelly 20
Sugar Plums... 6
Turkish Delight.................................... 8
White Chocolate Almond Bark 14

Cookies

Almond Biscotti.................................. 50
Angel Pillows...................................... 54
Apricot Frosting 54
Brown Sugar Shortbread 49
Brune Kager *(Danish Spice Cookies)*..... 43
Chocolate-Covered Cherry
  Cookies 57
Christmas Rum Balls......................... 12
Dapper Cookies................................... 55
Decorating Cookies &
  Houses.. 40, 42
Flarn 45
Ginger Shortbread 48
Gingerbread Cookies......................... 42
Holiday Hideaways 58
Holiday Spritz Cookies..................... 39
Holiday Sugar Cookies..................... 40
Icing Paint... 41
Kanel Kakor 44
Kourabiedes *(Greek Shortbread)*........... 47
Lemon Shortbread 48
Mexican Mocha Balls 53
Mom Mandryk's Christmas
  Nuggets 56
Orechove Kolieska Zlepovane
  (Czechoslovakian Raspberry Walnut
  Sandwiches) 46
Royal Icing.. 41
Shortbread Cookies 48, 49
Shortbread Wedges........................... 49
Sugar Biscuits..................................... 46
Traditional Scottish Shortbread....... 48
Whipped Shortbread......................... 48

Crafts

Christmas Dough Ornaments 24
Cinnamon Craft Ornaments............ 24
Decorating Cookies and
  Gingerbread houses............. 40, 41, 42
Marzipan Fruits, Vegetables
  and Figures 7

Desserts

Almond Cheesecake.......................... 157
Apple Bread Pudding with Maple
  Rum Sauce 154
Baked Alaska 162
Cherries Jubilee 163
Chocolate Crumb Crust 157, 158
Chocolate Curls................................. 159
Holiday Trifle..................................... 162
Mandarin Chocolate Cheesecake ... 158
Tiramisu.. 161
Vanilla Almond Crumb Crust......... 160
White Chocolate Strawberry
  Mousse Cake 160

Fillings, Glazes, Icings, Sauces, Toppings

Apricot Frosting 54
Blender Hollandaise 79
Brown Sugar and Mustard Glaze... 151
Brown Sugar Hard Sauce................. 29
Caramel Sauce 28
Caramel Topping 70
Chili Sauce.. 144
Chocolate Coating 10, 58
Cinnamon-Maple Syrup and
  Glaze 84
Cream Cheese Frosting..................... 39
Creamy Amaretto Filling................. 157
Creamy Chocolate Frosting 60
Creamy Custard Sauce 29
Ganache Glaze.................................... 158
Hollandaise Sauce............................. 79
Icing Paint... 41
Icing Sugar Glaze.............................. 37
Lemon Glaze....................................... 88
Maple Rum Sauce.............................. 154
Marzipan 90
Old-Fashioned Orange Sauce.......... 28
Onion Cream Sauce........................... 132
Orange Glaze...................................... 152
Parmesan Shrimp Sauce................... 124
Pineapple Glaze................................. 152
Pineapple Sauce................................. 72
Rhubarb Sauce.................................... 144

Fillings, Glazes, Icings, Sauces, Toppings (cont'd)

Royal Icing 41
Sherried Cream Sauce 148
Sour Cream Amaretto Topping 157
Sour Cream-Bacon Sauce 73
Spiced Hard Sauce 29
Traditional Hard Sauce 29
Triple Orange Filling 158
Vanilla Brandy sauce 154
White Chocolate Strawberry
    Filling 160

Main Dishes

Beef
Beef Wellington 146
Creamy Beef Stroganoff 145

Pork
Cranberry Stuffing for Pork
    Roast 142
Crown Roast of Pork 142
Perfect Baked Ham 151
Tourtière 143

Poultry:
Cheesy Turkey Bruschetta 135
Creamy Turkey and Spinach
    Tetrazzini 135
Duckling à l'Orange 139
Paella 141
Roast Christmas Goose 136
Roast Turkey with Mushroom
    Bread Stuffing 133
Rock Cornish Hens with
    Dressing 140
Spicy Turkey Chili 135
Turkey Broccoli Stir-Fry 135
Turkey Grape Salad 135
Turkey Tips & Leftovers 135

Seafood
Coquilles St. Jacques 149
Creamy Dilled Seafood
    Casserole 150
Smoked Salmon Lasagna 148

Stuffings
Cranberry Stuffing 142
Herbed Ground Beef Stuffing 134
Mixed Fruit Stuffing 136
Rice and Mushroom Dressing 140
Sausage Stuffing 134

Salads & Salad Dressings

Salad Dressings
Horseradish Garlic Mayonnaise ... 120
Peppery Mustard Dressing 119
Raspberry Vinaigrette 117
Red Wine Vinegar Dressing 118

Salads
Cashew and Orange Salad 118
Christmas Cranberry Apple
    Salad 114
Cranberry Sparkle Salad 114
Fire and Ice Tomatoes 119
Fresh Fruit Salad 116
Golden Glow Salad 115
Melon Basket 116
Oriental Shrimp Salad 120
Shrimp and Corn Salad 120
Tossed Greens with Raspberry
    Vinaigrette 117
Tropical Fruit Salad 116
Turkey Grape Salad 135

Soups
Christmas Sauerkraut Soup 110
French Canadian Pea Soup 110
French Onion Soup 111
Hearty Clam Chowder 112
Sherried Mushroom Soup 112

Vegetable Dishes
Cauliflower and Mushrooms in
    Cheese Sauce 123
Cauliflower Tomato Medley 125
Cauliflower with Shrimp Sauce 124
Corn-Mushroom Bake 126
Crunchy Broccoli 121
Dilled Cheesy Hash Browns 75
Golden Carrot Ring 127
Great Green Vegetable Bake, The ... 122
Green Vegetable Medley 122
Holiday Sweet Potatoes 128
Holiday Turnips 128
Potatoes Romanoff 129
Pyrohi 131
Sour Cabbage Rolls 132
Spinach Puff 126
Whipped Potato Casserole 130

Share A Taste of Christmas

Order A Taste of Christmas at $14.95 per book plus $3.00 (total order) for postage and handling.

Number of books_____ x $14.95 = $ ____
Shipping and handling charge _____ = $ _3.00_
Subtotal _____ = $ ____
In Canada add 7% GST_____ (Subtotal x .07) = $ ____
Total enclosed_____ = $ ____

U.S. and international orders payable in U.S. funds / Price is subject to change.

NAME: _____
STREET: _____
CITY:_____ PROV./STATE _____
COUNTRY_____ POSTAL CODE/ZIP ____

Please make cheque or money order payable to: **Three Sisters Publishing**
12234 – 49 Street
Edmonton, Alberta
Canada   T5W 3A8

For fund raising or volume purchase prices, contact
Three Sisters Publishing. Please allow 3-4 weeks for delivery.

❈ ❈ ❈ ❈ ❈ ❈ ❈ ❈ ❈ ❈ ❈ ❈ ❈ ❈ ❈ ❈ ❈ ❈

Share A Taste of Christmas

Order A Taste of Christmas at $14.95 per book plus $3.00 (total order) for postage and handling.

Number of books_____ x $14.95 = $ ____
Shipping and handling charge _____ = $ _3.00_
Subtotal _____ = $ ____
In Canada add 7% GST_____ (Subtotal x .07) = $ ____
Total enclosed_____ = $ ____

U.S. and international orders payable in U.S. funds / Price is subject to change.

NAME: _____
STREET: _____
CITY:_____ PROV./STATE _____
COUNTRY_____ POSTAL CODE/ZIP ____

Please make cheque or money order payable to: **Three Sisters Publishing**
12234 – 49 Street
Edmonton, Alberta
Canada   T5W 3A8

For fund raising or volume purchase prices, contact
Three Sisters Publishing. Please allow 3-4 weeks for delivery.

Order Form 171

❈ ❈ ❈ ❈ ❈ ❈ ❈ ❈ ❈ ❈ ❈ ❈ ❈ ❈ ❈ ❈ ❈ ❈